Norfolk Summer: Making
the Go-Between

Norfolk Summer: Making the Go-Between

Christopher Hartop

John Adamson
Cambridge 2011

First published 2011
John Adamson
90 Hertford Street
Cambridge CB4 3AQ

© 2011
Book: John Adamson
Text: Christopher Hartop
Images: as credited
Synopsis: Canal + Image UK Limited

Christopher Hartop has asserted his moral right to be identified as the author of this work.

ISBN 978-1-898565-07-9

British Library Cataloguing in Publication Data
A catalogue record of this book is available from the British Library

Every effort has been made by the author and publisher to contact the owners of the copyright of the images in this book.

Edited and produced by John Adamson
Designed by Chris Jones, Design4Science Ltd
Printed on Burgo R400 170 gsm paper by Conti Tipocolor, Florence, Italy

CONTENTS

FOREWORD

A COCKSURE YOUNG F. SCOTT FITZGERALD famously told the great D.W. Griffith that the best stories to film were the ones that took place behind the camera. This is not the case with *The Go-Between*, where the story is of such intensity that it moved Harold Pinter to tears when he first read it. Joseph Losey's screen version of the book, recognized as one of the great films of the twentieth century, can be viewed on several levels, but the story of how it came to the screen is nonetheless a story worth telling, too.

Unlike painting, or writing a novel, film-making is not a solitary activity. Of all artistic endeavours, the process of creation in film has still not been deconstructed into a single artist-craftsman working in the splendid isolation that seemed to be so important to John Ruskin. Even today, Hollywood makes films the old-fashioned way, in an industrial process no different from the workshops of the great *ébénistes* or silversmiths of eighteenth-century Paris. It is a process that relies on the specialist skills of many. But the fortuitous coming together of writer, director, actors and technicians, who essentially work as one, can produce a work of art as masterly as if it had been created with one mind and one pair of hands. It happens all too rarely in the cinema, but it did happen with *The Go-Between*.

Anyone who writes about Losey owes a great debt to David Caute, whose magisterial biography appeared in 1994. But in some respects I disagree with Caute's analysis of Losey as a man, which is so unflattering that it gets in the way of an assessment of his achievement. Losey was only happy when working, and he firmly believed that good films could also be commercially successful. Sadly, again and again throughout his career he was proved wrong, and nowadays the battle that Losey fought so valiantly seems to have been lost. Losey once reflected that cinema "is constantly hampered by those few who control its finance and distribution, so much so that there are few advances in the cinema comparable with those we have seen in music, painting or even literature". The handful of Losey's films that did combine great art with commercial success stand out like beacons from another age; among these, *The Go-Between* shines brightest.

Most importantly, I am grateful to Patricia Losey for her help and encouragement, for making available her unpublished diaries and memoir, and for allowing me to quote from them as well as from Joseph Losey's papers in the British Film Institute. I owe a particular debt to Terry Hodgkinson (2nd assistant director), who was an early and enthusiastic supporter of the project, as were Julia Hull (*née* Howlett), Roger Lloyd Pack, Miriam Rawlinson and Steve Smith.

I am especially grateful to the following for their help: Julie Christie, Edward Fox, Richard Gibson, Dominic Guard, John Heyman, Simon Hume-Kendall and David Stephenson. The following also gave up their time to be interviewed or generously offered information or help: Michael Barclay, Elspeth Barker, Raffaella Barker, Geraldine Bird, Marc Berlin, Sarah Bulwer-Long, Nigel Bumphrey, the late Michael Gough, Simon Gough, Peter Hammond, Dominick Harrod, Pauline Harrold, Lizzie Harvey, Elizabeth Howard, Susan Howard, Joshua Losey, Jeremy Meanley, Nobby Mitchell, David Riddington, William Stebbings, Catherine Webster and Margaret Webster.

I am also grateful to the following for permission to publish extracts from published works or unpublished letters and other material: Michael Bloch and David Higham Associates Ltd (diaries of James Lees-Milne), Judy Daish Associates (Harold Pinter), Lisa Dowdeswell of the Society of Authors (L.P. Hartley), Anneke Wills (from her books *Self Portrait* and *Naked*) and Adrian Wright (from his book *Another Country*).

I received great help from Massimo Moretti of Optimum Releasing/Studio Canal Ltd, Johnny Davies (Special Collections) and David McCall (Stills Collection), British Film Institute, and from Katherine Manger of the East Anglian Film Archive.

It has, as always, been a pleasure to work with Chris Jones of Design4Science and the team at Conti Tipocolor. John Adamson, the trusted pilot, has brought this vessel clear of the rocks and into the harbour and to him I am especially grateful. My wife Juliet has been my inspiration and it is to her that I dedicate this book.

Christopher Hartop

1 SUMMER'S DAY

Norfolk to the north of Norwich is not flat but a landscape of gently rolling hills, dotted here and there with an ancient tree or a small wood masking a marl pit. On the horizon rise square, or round, church towers. It is a patchwork of fields which turns from dark brown to green to gold with the seasons in a rhythm that speaks of countless generations of people who lived here and worked the soil. This part of Norfolk has been called timeless. But surely it is *timeful*? Can the past co-exist with the present?

Wednesday, August 26, 1970
Thornage Common, north Norfolk

8:00 am

The sun has been up for a couple of hours as a pantechnicon lorry carefully edges its way off the road onto the grass verge. The doors open to reveal half a dozen men, some seasoned professionals, others local brawn. They start unloading large lights, setting them up by a cricket pavilion.

A straggling settlement strung along a winding road, Thornage in reality has no cricket pitch, but its common has been chosen by the makers of *The Go-Between* because the row of unspoilt period cottages along its southern side will make a picturesque backdrop to the action of a cricket

1. Edward Fox (Viscount Trimingham) prepares to bowl.

match. Carmen Dillon, the film's seasoned art director, spent weeks driving around Norfolk scouting locations, but the final decision to use Thornage for the cricket-match scene was made by John Southwood, the location manager, shortly before shooting began last month. Frequent mowing over the past weeks has brought the grass to something resembling the manicured greensward of a real pitch.

Other than the removal of a few television aerials, the village houses have needed little alteration to make them look authentic for the year 1900. Most importantly, though, Thornage is only a few miles

"I certainly feel more and more that the past is not past, that it never was past. It's present" Harold Pinter, 1971

from Melton Constable Hall where the crew are based. The film is on a tight budget, but time is also in short supply. Rain and wind last week had forced the crew to abandon any idea of shooting the cricket scene according to the schedule, and they had retreated instead into the hall at Melton to do interior scenes. An innovation of *The Go-Between* is that every scene of the film is being shot on location in Norfolk, and the disused seventeenth-century mansion has been transformed by Dillon and her team into a perfect version of a late Victorian house, with tables crowded with bric-à-brac and hundreds of pictures covering the walls. Joseph Losey, the director, is adamant that everything in the film should be authentic. The antique shops along the coast road have been ransacked for relics of everyday life of seventy years earlier; finding a seedsman's advertising calendar of 1900 in a junk shop in Aylsham was particularly gratifying. But the interior scenes are running out and some of the cast members are nearing the end of their contracts. The cricket match between the gentry from the hall and the local village team, involving virtually the entire cast and needing a huge quantity of extras as players and spectators, is the great set piece of the movie, and it is now or never.

The summer so far has been grey and somewhat wet – in stark contrast to the July heat-wave required by the script. In the screenplay, young Leo Colston swelters in his suit as each day he watches the mercury rise to new highs. But how to create baking sun when the weather is cool and windy? One of the scenes, of the family and house guests bathing in a lake, will be filmed at Hickling Broad on a cool blustery day. The greyness of the water, reflecting the leaden sky, and the wind rippling its surface will be impossible to mask, but brilliant use of sound by the recording engineer Peter Handford, who will in due course replace the roar of the wind with the hum of insects punctuated by bird calls, will give the scene its feeling of summer heat. The cricket match is also scripted to take place on a hot, sunny day. But will the sun oblige today?

Meanwhile, at Melton Constable Hall, several buses filled with locals, enlisted from the neighbouring villages through advertisements in local newspapers, disgorge a cross-section of 1970 Norfolk, who become a 1900 Norfolk crowd in no time at all. Camilla Farmer, the costume co-ordinator, has been up since dawn sorting a varied selection of old and new clothing that transforms each villager into his or her late Victorian forebear. One of them, Fleming Cooper, was ten years old in 1900 and may well have witnessed a similar cricket match as a boy. The gardener at the hall, George Grieff of Brinton, dons a bowler hat and gaiters, as does Fred Holmes. Among the villagers are Lorna Bunn, Thornage's postmistress, and Joyce Lord, the vicar's wife. As the extras board their buses again to go on to Thornage, Camilla can turn her attention to the cast members.

Julie Christie has been picked up at 6:30 am from the house she is renting near Aylsham, some ten miles away, by Steve, the unit driver, and driven to Melton for costume fitting. Margaret Leighton, staying in the genteel grandeur of the Hotel de Paris in the seaside resort of Cromer with her husband, the fellow actor Michael Wilding, has arrived at the hall by taxi. Other cast and crew have made their own way to Melton by car or bicycle from the houses they are occupying in nearby villages. Alan Bates has left his wife and baby at Bale Hall a few miles away. A cheery group of hairdressers and make-up artists, renting a house in Hindolveston, have squashed themselves into a Mini and gone straight to Thornage to set themselves up in the cricket

Alan Bates (Ted Burgess) outside the impromptu cricket pavilion.

pavilion. Losey spurns the heavy, theatrical make-up of studio-made films. He has even made Margaret Leighton discard her false eyelashes for the film. Unable to bear this injunction, a few days ago she put on a small pair, hoping he would not notice "Your eye lashes have grown in the night, Maggie," he growled.

Losey and Harold Pinter, the film's screenwriter, have been driven straight to Thornage from Brancaster on the coast, a full hour's drive away. Losey and his girlfriend Patricia, whom he will marry in King's Lynn Registry Office after the filming is completed, are renting Marsh Barn on the edge of the marshes at Brancaster and Pinter comes to stay with them from time to time. He arrived last week and, after the cricket scene was postponed, has hung on, watching the filming of interior scenes, and each evening he and Losey have viewed the previous day's rushes in the impromptu cinema set up in a room at Melton. Patricia has noted in her diary: "The weather is grey, cold, misty and shows no sign of clearing".

Obsessive about cricket, Pinter is keen to see his meticulously accurate depiction of the match turned into film. "Cricket was very much a part of my life from the day I was born," Pinter once quipped. For some years now Pinter has played for the Gaieties, a theatrical team founded by the music-hall star Lupino Lane. Fred Paolozzi, a team mate from the Gaieties, has just arrived and like Pinter has donned cricket gear, for both men are to be fielders. To lend a further touch of authenticity, cricketers from the area have been enlisted, among them Oliver Barnes, biology master at Gresham's School in nearby Holt, and Ron Bell, who has played for Norfolk. Stephen Bush and Stanley Page, also respected local cricketers, are to act as umpires. The equipment too is real, on loan from Slazenger's in return for a mention in the film credits.

The producer "Spike" Priggen and the location manager John Southwood discuss the weather.

9:00 am

Most of the cast have now arrived at Thornage, blocking the nearby lanes with cars and vans. The wooden pavilion is buzzing with people having their make-up applied. Southwood and "Spike" Priggen, the producer, eye the structure nervously. It is in reality a chicken battery of bolted panels and still with its ventilators in the roof. A couple of pre-fabricated windows have been inserted into the front. (Afterwards Priggen will offer it to the village but, unable to get planning permission for a permanent structure, the parish council will turn it down and it will be carted away, leaving the cricket pitch to return to meadow.)

Richard Dalton, the 1st assistant director, and Gerry Gavigan, the 3rd assistant, stay at Losey's elbow as the technicians set up the camera and size up a few shots. Terry Hodgkinson, the 2nd assistant director, keeps in touch with them by army surplus walkie-talkie as he arranges the villagers around the pitch. Some of the extras are told to climb aboard a farm wagon to watch the action.

*Cast and crew relax on
Thornage Common.*

The hall team is dressed in spotless white flannels
while the village team, headed by Alan Bates as the
farmer Ted Burgess, wear more motley gear. The
family from the hall and their guests, the men in
gaily striped blazers and straw hats and the women
in elegant long dresses, twirling their parasols, sit in
period deck-chairs outside the pavilion. Miriam
Rawlinson from nearby Stody Hall, playing one of
the house guests, has brought along her two little
girls and her sister-in-law Sarah Bulwer-Long, all of
them elegant in summery dresses and broad-
brimmed hats. A local boy, Ian Darricott, clad in
a sailor suit, walks around asking the cast for
their autographs.

10:00 am

Organizing the crowds comes easily to Terry
Hodgkinson, who has just returned from a five-year
stint in Spain, much of it spent marshalling troops
of local gypsies, playing American Indians, for
spaghetti westerns. Filming requires a military
approach, and for virtually all of the participants
it involves endless waiting, as in any military
operation. Now, they are waiting for the sun to come
out. The extras give free flight to their imagination
and relish being in costume; they walk about clearly
savouring being part of this turn-of-the-century
scene. The cast, in contrast, shed as much of their
costumes as they can, putting on modern garments,
and sit in deck-chairs with their names emblazoned
on the backs, or lounge on the grass. Margaret
Leighton is invited into Julia Howlett's house on the
edge of the common for a cup of tea and the
chance to discard some of her costume. Julia drove
her pony and trap over to the hall at Melton on the
first day's shooting, thinking the crew might rent
them and was instead taken on to appear as one of
the maids in the film. Not needed for the cricket

*Miriam Rawlinson with
her two daughters,
Joanna and Nicola.*

Terry Hodgkinson, 2nd assistant director.

Beatty and also been lukewarm about her last film *Petulia*, made two years before. A week from now, however, she will agree to speak to an Anglia Television reporter, but in the screened footage her tension will be apparent.

Joseph Losey has also invited guests to watch the day's shooting. The Dean of Norwich, Alan Webster, who allowed the company to film in the cathedral, watches the proceedings with his wife while Catherine, their ten-year-old daughter, sits down next to Julie Christie and asks her to sign a book. Billa Harrod, wife of the economist Sir Roy Harrod and friend of L.P. Hartley, the author of *The Go-Between*, arrives with her son Dominick and casts a critical eye over the authenticity of the costumes and settings. She approves.

The elderly Earl of Leicester, immaculate in white trousers and shoes, blue blazer and boater, has been driven over from Holkham Hall in his black Bentley. "I am not one of the extras," he explains to a reporter, "but I thought I should dress the part for the visit". He will later tell Losey that he was bitterly disappointed not to have been included in any of the shots: "Didn't you see I came correctly dressed in my father's cricket clothes?" The prospect of having a cup of tea with Julie Christie, though, will more than compensate, for he has developed a crush on the actress. He will try, unsuccessfully, to entice her for dinner at Holkham.

scenes, she has been helping today as a go-between herself between the unit and the local residents, some of whom have been reluctant to take down their television aerials. While waiting, Julie Christie plays a board game with Julia's boyfriend, Willem Ekels, who is Michael Gough's stand-in. Julia does not mind but a few days later when Willem is invited to lunch at Julie's house in Burgh-next-Aylsham, she will be uneasy. She should not worry, for Christie's boyfriend Warren Beatty will be there too, bringing a whiff of Hollywood glamour to the tiny village.

The throng on the pitch has been swelled by onlookers. Local residents who have had no interest in being in the film themselves have been nevertheless drawn to the spectacle. The road along the edge of the common has been closed for the day, yet passers-by seem to appear from nowhere. A reporter and photographer from the *Eastern Daily Press* arrive, followed by a news crew from Anglia Television, who will shoot silent 16mm black-and-white footage to be shown as a back-drop to the evening's newscast. For the first couple of weeks of filming, the set at Melton had been closed to the press and now, seven weeks into shooting, all journalists still have to be vetted by the producer. Julie Christie allows no interviews. She is wary of the press, who for years have charted the ups and downs of her tempestuous relationship with Warren

Left to right: Richard Gibson (Marcus), Jane Clarke (house guest), Willem Ekels (Michael Gough's stand-in, who also played one of the scorers in the cricket match scene), unidentified, Julie Christie (Marian).

TEA ON THE GREEN

The Earl of Leicester and Julie Christie take tea outside the cricket pavilion. From the Eastern Daily Press, August 27, 1970.

11:00 am

The tension felt by the crew, only too aware that time is passing and the sun has yet to come out, echoes the underlying drama of the scene to be filmed, where the hall team is captained by Lord Trimingham, the local landowner and Marian's fiancé, and the villagers are led in the batting by Ted Burgess, with whom Marian is having a secret affair. But such dramas, real or literary, largely pass the extras and spectators by. They are caught in a dream of a late Victorian summer's day, even though the sky is cloudy. "I enjoyed living in someone else's imagination," Elspeth Barker, wife of the poet George Barker, will reminisce years later. She responded to one of the advertisements and has been taken on as one of the villagers along with Raffaella, her five-and-a-half-year-old daughter. In her reverie, Elspeth tries to understand what the big folk are doing and talking about – past and present, commingled.

The cricketers practise languidly. Anneke Wills, wife of Michael Gough, has brought their son Jasper over from the house they are renting at Cley and they all sit watching with Edward Fox, Anneke's old boyfriend from their RADA days. Alan Bates shows Julie Christie how to hold a bat. Some of the village men gather around an urn supplied by Mr Cook, the

Still from an Anglia Television news clip of the cricket match. On the right are Elspeth Barker and her daughter Raffaella.

Michael Gough (Mr
Maudsley) and his wife
Anneke Wills, left, and
their son Jasper, with
Edward Fox at right.

caterer, and drink tea out of paper cups. "Have you ever been to London, George?" one of them is asked. "Noo," he replies, "but oi've bin t'Peterborough." Elspeth Barker's two-and-a-half-year-old son escapes from his baby-sitter and runs onto the pitch. "We'd better put that child in costume," says Losey. Spike Priggen wanders about with a cup of coffee, casting anxious glances up at the sky.

11:30 am
The sight of Losey having his hair trimmed by Stephanie Kaye, the chief hairdresser, belies the

tension. Suddenly the sun comes out. The crew snaps into action. "Quiet please, we're shooting," shouts Gerry Gavigan. "Who are they shooting, Mummy?" asks little Jasper Gough. For the bowling scenes the camera has been enclosed in a specially built hide with a plate-glass front, positioned to film the batsman from silly mid on. Pinter's screenplay has outlined a series of short takes of the batting by the hall team: *Trimingham driving gracefully. Trimingham cutting. Trimingham glancing to leg*. It is decided that the takes are too technical and need to be simplified. Pinter strikes them out of his copy of the script.

Ron Bell bowls and Fox, an experienced cricketer in real life, bats forcefully. One ball shatters a milk bottle off camera between Alan Bates and Pinter, echoing the ball in the film flogged by Ted Burgess which crashes onto the pavilion roof and bounces among the lady spectators from the hall. "Mrs Maudsley! Are you all right?" exclaims the rector.

A momentary distraction to the shooting is provided by one of the lady extras who has a wasp trapped inside her voluminous Victorian skirt and is stung "high on the leg" as the *Eastern Daily Press* will elegantly record it the next day.

It is hot. In years to come, cast and crew alike will remember those weeks of filming *The Go-Between* in the summer of 1970 as a heat-wave. In one's memory it is easy to confuse the film with the reality, for the cloudy days will have far outnumbered the sunny ones. Past and present, film and reality merge.

Joseph Losey has his hair
trimmed by Stephanie
Kaye; duty nurse on the
right.

Overleaf: Julie Christie
and Alan Bates relax
between takes on
Thornage Common.

*Alan Bates bats, Roger
Lloyd Pack (Charles) is
wicket-keeper, Simon
Hume-Kendall (Denys),
second from the left,
is fielding.*

2:00 pm

It is time to shoot the scenes of Edward Fox bowling as Alan Bates bats. Unlike Fox, Bates is no cricketer but he has been given coaching by the real players. Having learnt to play the flute for *Far from the Madding Crowd,* and judo for *Women in Love*, Bates will add not only cricket but also singing to his repertoire during the shooting of *The Go-Between*. Skilful cutting between shots of Bates at the wicket and Fox bowling will manage to give the impression of Ted Burgess repeatedly hitting six with animal vigour. As they rehearse, Fox bowls and hits Bates in the hand. Worried that it might swell up and spoil the shot, Spike Priggen calls over Dr Meanley of Melton Constable to examine it. No bones appear to have been broken, but he suggests that an x-ray be taken in Holt after filming is completed for the day. Dalton makes notes of the incident for the day's report which Terry Hodgkinson will prepare that evening back at Melton Constable.

On the cart where half a dozen local men sit, smoking pipes and watching the action, Peter Handford has positioned a microphone which discreetly records their comments. Months later, at Elstree Studios, Hertfordshire, he and the editor, Reginald Beck, will weave these snippets of Norfolk dialect into a backdrop to the shots of the match. Life and art, past and present merge.

5:00 pm

The sunlight has started to lose its intensity but most of the shots of the batting have been done. The camera has been taken out of its hide to take shots of fielders catching or fumbling some of Ted Burgess's balls filmed earlier. The shaking of hands between the two teams, which takes place at the beginning of the match, is filmed from a low angle. More scenes of dialogue and the reactions of the spectators will be taken tomorrow. The day has gone well after all and Losey is satisfied. Soft-spoken and thoughtful, he is an efficient director who will deliver the film on time and within budget. With few words he has inspired the actors and crew.

The actors and extras go back to Melton Constable to change. Groups of them gravitate to pubs close by: the Bell in Hunworth, or the Feathers in Holt.

The crew carefully pack up; for some of them the day is not over. Back at the hall, the call sheet for tomorrow has to be prepared by Hodgkinson and given to Sally O'Neill, the production secretary, to type up and mimeograph. The time that each performer and crew member is required on set, what scenes will be shot (with alternatives in case of bad weather), what props will be required, what costumes. He will distribute the foolscap sheets to everyone, jumping into his 2CV and taking them to those who have already left. Then the daily report will be typed up: what scenes were shot; how many feet of film. The undeveloped film is handed to Bob Whitaker, glamorous photographer renowned for his images of the Vietnam war and the Beatles, who has been spending a few days taking photographs of the shoot for a feature in *Vogue*. He roars away from the hall in his red Scimitar bound for London, where he will drop the film off in Soho to be developed before heading on to a party. Losey and Pinter settle down with some of the crew to watch yesterday's rushes. Later they will drive back to Brancaster to join Patricia and Losey's twelve-year-old son Joshua for a late supper. Losey will go over the scenes for tomorrow's shooting and make notes. 1900 will be played out again at Thornage.

2011

The houses along the common look essentially the same. Some belong to weekenders and their window frames are painted now with Farrow and Ball colours, but no one looks out of the windows during the week. Passers-by have to slow down at the bend as they drive past. Some, perhaps, when they see the meadow remember a cricket match played there in 1900.

2 LON_G Road

WHEN L.P. HARTLEY'S ELEGANTLY WRITTEN NOVEL of lost childhood innocence appeared in 1953, the critics, led by Evelyn Waugh, were unanimous in their acclaim. The book's economical style lent itself to film adaptation, and its sexual tension, and nuances of class and period – the book is set in 1900 – all seemed to promise box-office success. Shortly after its publication, Hartley sold the film rights to the film producer Alexander Korda. Talk was widespread of an adaptation to be directed by the aristocratic veteran Anthony "Puffin" Asquith but several years passed and no film emerged. Looking back years later, Hartley asserted, "Korda never meant to make a film of the book; that's what annoyed me. He just bought it to keep as a property, thinking it might go up in market value. I was so annoyed when I learned this that I put a curse upon him, and he died, almost the next morning".[1] A more likely explanation of Korda's actions is that he realized that the book's climax, in which the two lovers, Marian and Ted, are witnessed making love by Marian's mother and the thirteen-year-old Leo, would not get past the censors in Britain or America without resorting to coy artifice. Hartley's gentle image of "a shadow on the wall that opened and closed like an umbrella" may not have been enough for film audiences in the mid-1950s, but mainstream cinema was not ready for "two bodies moving like one".

Joseph Losey (1907–1984). The director fought for seven years to bring L.P. Hartley's novel The Go-Between *to the screen.*

After Korda's death in 1956, the rights to the book were acquired for £8,000 by Robert Velaise, a flamboyant Swiss entrepreneur, who announced his intention to make the film. Velaise had made a fortune acquiring cinema chains in Europe and later in midtown Manhattan, and his lifestyle combined the glamour of Hollywood with European sophistication. But Velaise was not a film maker and he had no track record for raising production financing.

"There does seem to be a *hoodoo* on the film" L.P. Hartley, 1964

It is here that Joseph Losey enters the story. A mid-Westerner, born in Wisconsin, he had worked in left-wing theatre in the 1930s and made a name for himself as a careful craftsman of propaganda films in Hollywood in the 1940s. He had fled to London in 1953 to evade a subpoena from the House Committee on Un-American Activities that requested that he answer questions about his Communist connections. The infamous "Blacklist" during that time of hysteria prevented many Hollywood writers and directors from working in the United States. In Britain, Losey had found a more tolerant atmosphere – the trade unions were for the most part sympathetic to exiles from Cold War America – and he had joined the small band of American expatriate artists. At first he had worked on television scripts, largely as a result of Carl Foreman's help. Foreman, too, was a McCarthy-era exile, who before being blacklisted had enjoyed tremendous success in Hollywood with his screenplay for *High Noon* in 1951. In London, Foreman had continued to submit scripts to Hollywood under various *noms de plume*. When one of them, his screenplay for *The Bridge over the River Kwai*, won an Academy Award for best adaptation in 1956, Foreman had had to endure the farce of the Oscar being presented in Hollywood to the French author of the original book, Pierre Boulle, who spoke no English.

With Foreman's help, Losey had forged a network of contacts like "Puffin" Asquith and in 1954 he had been engaged to direct his first feature film in England, *The Sleeping Tiger*. As a precaution, he had used the pseudonym Victor Hanbury. Towards the end of the 1950s, however, as the influence of the Un-American Committee began to wane in the United States, Losey had found more work in England and began to develop an elegant, almost painterly, approach to film direction. With his 1957 film, *The Gypsy and the Gentleman*, he had turned a clunky costume pot-boiler into a riot of stylish scenes, replete with imagery, inspired by Rowlandson and Hogarth. But apart from these occasional flashes of brilliance, Losey's work in the 1950s gives little indication of the mastery of his later films, where he moved away from his Hollywood roots towards a more continental European approach.

Robert Velaise (1914–2011), with Marlene Dietrich, c. 1950. Swiss by birth, Velaise developed chains of cinemas in Europe and later in New York. He acquired the film rights to The Go-Between *after Alexander Korda's death in 1956.*

Velaise, who had commissioned Paul Dehn to write a screenplay for *The Go-Between*, made overtures to Losey. Dehn had worked with "Puffin" Asquith in the 1950s and would go on to establish a reputation for writing *The Spy who Came in from the Cold* (1965) and taut action films such as *Goldfinger* (1964). One can only suppose that his screenplay, which does not appear to have survived, faithfully followed the book within the conventions laid down by Hollywood. But it soon became clear that potential backers were reluctant to finance a film to be produced by Velaise, or to be directed by Losey, still a stranger to big-budget productions. Matters drifted along. In the meantime Hartley had sold the dramatic rights to the book to H.M. Tennant, the theatrical producers, in a deal which would later cause considerable problems.

Around this time, Losey met the playwright Harold Pinter. Here began a collaboration that would drastically change Losey's art and also open up for Pinter new avenues in a medium he had hitherto not explored. Although Pinter's first three plays, *The Room*, *The Birthday Party* and *The Dumb Waiter*, all produced in 1957, had had a disastrous reception by audiences and critics alike, all three plays contained elements of a new approach that would earn Pinter critical acclaim only a few years later. Pinter was moving theatre into new, uncharted waters, and it was *The Caretaker*, opening in 1959, which saw his meteoric rise to artistic as well as commercial success.

In Pinter, Losey saw the possibility of collaboration with a writer who could take cinema away from what he saw as Hollywood banality. Pinter was fascinated by words and their ambiguities, and how they could be used to set up barriers between people rather than as a vehicle of communication. Words, presented with Losey's lavish direction, could dumbfound and perplex audiences.

In April, 1960, Losey had written to Pinter congratulating him on his television play *A Night Out*, and intimated to Pinter's agent that he would be interested in discussing a film script. The outcome was *The Servant*, which Pinter adapted from Robin Maugham's book and Losey directed in 1963. The film, starring Dirk Bogarde, James Fox and Wendy Craig, won three British Academy Film Awards and was commercially successful too, proving, Losey felt, that a film could be both an artistic and a commercial triumph.

Losey and Pinter would go on to produce two more films of international stature, catapulting Losey into the firmament of artistic cinema, and allowing Pinter to hone his dramatic skills in a new medium, thereby bringing his art to a much wider audience. No sooner was *The Servant* completed, in October 1963, than Losey asked Pinter to read *The Go-Between*. He did, and later said: "[I]t had such a tremendous impact on me that I actually broke down. Nothing less than tears".[2] Pinter maintained he could not turn such an exquisite book into a screenplay: "It's too painful, too perfect", he protested. But Losey talked him into it, and within six months Pinter had produced a screenplay.[3] Losey was delighted with the result, and wrote to tell Hartley that it was "quite brilliant and absolutely in its terms and forms matches the perfection of your book".

Leslie Hartley was by then well into his sixties and regarded as a literary figure of the old school. His prodigious output as an editor and critic had complemented his work on his own novels, which he wrote during long sojourns in Venice. Hartley's initial reaction to the idea of having Pinter adapt *The Go-Between* for the screen had been negative: taken to a Pinter double bill, afterwards "his head flopped not at all appreciatively ...

signalling that he didn't know what the theatre was coming to".[4] Later, he confided to a friend that he had heard that Losey was "very left-wing". But Losey and Pinter managed to convince this old-fashioned bachelor that their approach would be sympathetic to the themes of his book and its nuances. When Hartley read the first part of Pinter's draft screenplay he was delighted: "I think Pinter's script is splendid … He has seen all my points, and added a good many of his own. Do please give him my congratulations. Surely we can do something to break down the frustrating influence of Mr V! … I think the dialogue between the two boys is particularly good – and in some strange way Pinter has succeeded in making the dialogue in general up-to-date (which mine isn't) without losing its old-world flavour. He has caught the country-house-party feeling beautifully and is so sensitive to the nuances of rank and condition and degree, which are very important to the story. Nor does he miss a dramatic development …" In fact, Hartley's novel is a classic of the "tight" style that Waugh and others had developed in the middle decades of the century, and its dialogue is Pinter-like in its deceptive simplicity.

Losey was determined to put together financing for the film and if possible buy out Velaise, who was still trying to get financing himself for a production with Asquith as director. The impresario Lew (later Lord) Grade was approached by Losey, and at Grade's suggestion Robin Fox, Losey's friend and agent, approached Velaise, who later recalled: "I told him 'I'm not in the business of buying and selling rights. I bought the rights to make the film', whereupon he [Fox] said, 'But you can't make the film,' so I said, 'O.K. then I won't make it, but neither will anybody else. Either it will be made by me or nobody else'".[5] Grade and Fox then encouraged Hartley to work on a stage version of the book in an attempt to scare Velaise, as any stage or television version would have made financing a movie version impossible. Velaise responded by buying the residual rights from Tennant's, the theatrical producers.

But Velaise went even further in this game of chess: he sued Hartley, alleging that he held an indefinite right to renew his rights on payment of £250 a year. The case proceeded slowly. Grade maintained that he would only back the project if a court ruled that Hartley controlled all the rights and could assign them to their project. Everything seemed mired in contradictory legal opinions. Hartley wrote pathetically to Losey in March, 1964: "I am so sorry about this, but there does seem to be a hoodoo on the film …"

But Losey refused to give up. There was nothing to be done but make Velaise an offer he could not refuse. On December 6, 1964 Losey was writing to Hartley: "[T]here are at least two set-ups prepared to finance *The Go-Between* immediately and completely if a situation can be found in which Harold Pinter and you and I can function". As for Velaise, "nobody seems willing to enter into financial arrangements with him, but they are willing to pay him handsomely for his nuisance value and to give him various important credits as a salve to his pride".[6] Getting wind of this, Paul Dehn contacted Losey about his own screenplay. Losey responded, "I am sure you are aware that I never lost my interest in doing the G-B. After my collaboration with Harold Pinter on *The Servant* many things have happened. In the first place, I have leapt ahead in my particular style and development, and, secondly, I have discovered the enormous satisfaction and joy in working with Pinter. Without going into more detail, which I can if and when we ever meet again, for these reasons and for many others I became progressively less interested in your version of the G-B and more interested in a new approach of my own and Harold Pinter's …" Losey could not resist a sting in the tail: "Perhaps I should say that, just as you undoubtedly are aware of my interests and activities, so I have been at all times aware of your continuing interest, and of your continuing activities with Puffin Asquith and with Velaise".

Financing, however, still eluded Losey. It was not only, it seems, the legal problems surrounding the rights to the book that made backers reluctant to open their cheque books. Losey, who had fought bitterly with the producers of his 1962 film, *Eve*, the brothers Robert and Raymond Hakim, and the backers of *The Servant*, had acquired a reputation of being "difficult". To most actors, Losey was a god – sympathetic and quiet without being dictatorial. But, as one friend put it, Losey had "a problem with authority" and increasingly he saw the money men and their commercial demands coming between his art and the public.

Nevertheless, the creative partnership between Losey and Pinter continued to flourish. Pinter produced an adaptation of Nicholas Mosley's novel *Accident*, which Losey directed in 1966. The film was released early the following year to widespread acclaim – and commercial success. Pinter, now a hot ticket both critically and financially, offered to pay Hartley's legal expenses in his law suit with Velaise. But *The Go-Between* continued to be cursed, as deal after deal fell through. Meanwhile, Losey took on other film projects; Pinter continued his stage work. *The Servant* and *Accident* had made Losey a national hero in France, where appreciation for film as art was far greater than in England or the United States. He became more and more European – in his outlook, his technique, his clothes, and his work became increasingly baroque – lush, full of rich imagery and set pieces. At times, such as in *Modesty Blaise* (1966) or *Boom* (1968), this could border on the camp. But elements of some of the style he showed in these films, as well as in *Secret Ceremony* (1968), were to be used with great success when he did finally come to direct *The Go-Between*.

Things began to look up in April 1968, when Losey wrote to Hartley: "[F]or the first time in years, I am encouraged to believe that the matter may be happily settled soon". Velaise had grown tired of litigation, but, more importantly, he had realized that he stood little chance of securing financing on his own. In the meantime, Losey's career was on a roll; he rivalled Visconti and Fellini as the most fêted director in Europe. His film *Boom*, an adaptation of Tennessee Williams's play *The Milk Train Doesn't Stop Here Any More*, starring Elizabeth Taylor and Richard Burton, was about to be released. A chance remark of Taylor's at Rex Harrison's Sardinian villa that she would like to play Mrs Goforth in the film had swept Losey up into the slipstream of the Burtons – a jet-set life of yachts, villas and glamour. It was a relationship that would last only a few films but it had the short-term effect of making Losey a bankable package. No matter that *Boom* would be panned by the critics and bomb at the box office, Losey had entered a new world.

Just as importantly, a new producer had entered his life, John Heyman, who ran World Film Services. Heyman was a respected operator adept at getting financing, especially from New York and Hollywood, and his approach with Losey was to let him get on with the job of making the film, while relying on Norman "Spike" Priggen to keep things on schedule and within budget. Priggen, an ex-soldier who had cut his teeth on such classics as *Kind Hearts and Coronets* and *The Cruel Sea*, had worked with Losey on his last five films. He was "tough but without artistic pretensions", as Dirk Bogarde remembers, "just what Joe needed".[7] In the meantime, Heyman could shield Losey from encounters with the dreaded backers. Velaise was ready to make a deal, to receive a screen credit as Executive Producer in return for a sizeable cash payment and his agreement effectively to walk away from the project.

At the beginning of the summer, Losey and Pinter revisited Pinter's screenplay and decided that it needed to be rewritten. Nearly five years had passed, during which both of them had had time to reflect. Pinter had become fascinated with time: on its most basic level, how the past could continue to influence a life many years later. A few years later, in his play *Old Times*, Pinter would go further to explore how a past can be created as a weapon of psychological domination. In *The Go-Between*, the traumatic effect of events in Leo Colston's childhood would blight the rest of his life, making him incapable of loving another human being. But was time really linear? Could it be composed of layers? Could the past co-exist with the present? Hartley's book deals with the effect of the past on the present with a simple narrative solution: it opens with a present-day (early 1950s) prologue which introduces a long flashback to the events of 1900; then returns to the present with a brief epilogue. Pinter offered a different approach: in his re-write, he interwove past and present, and suggested laying sounds of the present over visuals of the past, and vice versa. In a *New York Times* interview in 1971, Pinter explained: "I certainly feel more and more that the past is not past, that it never was past. It's present".[8]

What would unsettle cinema goers was the fact that the present-day scenes of old Leo are scrambled and not presented chronologically throughout the narrative. In doing this, Pinter turns conventional flashbacks on their heads: in Hollywood it was acceptable to present flashbacks out of chronological sequence (for example, as differently remembered sequences explaining events in the past), but to scramble present time, while presenting the past as a continuum, was shocking.[9]

Meanwhile, Losey lent his own thoughts to the look and feel of the film, and gave Pinter copious notes. Losey felt that the 1900 scenes should evoke the past so intensely that one became totally immersed in it. Complete authenticity was key. Losey wanted viewers to breathe it, to feel it as if they were there. In this, Losey was departing from the traditional, artificial, way in which the past was depicted in film and on television. In a theatrical tradition that went back to Shakespeare, the past had been suggested by impressionistic sets and costumes that were often wildly anachronistic. The sheer artificiality of it all seemed to invite the actors to over-act, so that the past was indeed a "foreign country", where everything is fake and bears no relation to reality. In films, this studio tradition where even the present is manufactured, later satirized by François Truffaut in his 1973 film *Day for Night* (*La Nuit américaine*), was to be replaced with complete authenticity, shot entirely on location. In the party scene in the village hall, the beer must be real; the collect read in the family prayer scene must be authentic and the right one for the day. The actors must inhabit the past, not a set.

By August 1968 Heyman was confident that financing would be forthcoming and plans were made to begin shooting the following July. Losey explained to the ever-eager Hartley that Richard MacDonald would be the art director. MacDonald and Losey had had a creative partnership going back to *The Sleeping Tiger* in 1954. He had designed *Eve*, Losey's 1962 florid and preposterous story of a Welsh writer in Italy, and had gone on to work with Losey on most of the latter's films in the 1960s. For *King and Country* (1964), MacDonald had invoked the muddy trenches of World War I by filling a studio at Shepperton with mud and a dead donkey. But by the late 1960s MacDonald was difficult to keep under control and constantly running foul of the unions. On the set of *Boom*, filming was interrupted when the simultaneous arrival of two current girlfriends and his wife drove MacDonald into hiding for several days. In the end, MacDonald had accepted a job in California and so was unavailable for *The Go-Between*, but he would be hired to do the titles.

24

Losey had carefully cultivated Leslie Hartley's friendship during the years of waiting, often taking him out to dinner and keeping him informed of the efforts being made to find financing. Hartley in turn had grown to appreciate both Losey's and Pinter's vision for the film. In a letter to Losey in August, 1968 Hartley explained the genesis of the book, which he said was based on his own Norfolk experiences as an adolescent staying in 1913 at Bradenham Hall, a house belonging to the Rider Haggard family which was rented out to "some well-to-do coal merchants called Moxey: their son was my school-friend, who asked me to stay". Hartley's memory evidently failed him, for the visit in fact took place four years earlier, when Hartley was thirteen. He had written to his mother from Bradenham on August 16, 1909: "I was met by Moxey in a motor-car, along with a chauffeur and a dog ... On Saturday we had a ball, very grand indeed, at least, not very. We always have late dinner here. There is going to be a cricket match today, the Hall against the village ..." Years later, after his mother's death, Hartley is said to have removed the letter from her papers, remarking that "this could make a story". As a result, the letter was not burnt along with the rest of their voluminous correspondence after his death.[10]

With Losey's notes at his side, Pinter worked on his rewrite of the screenplay: writing from Central Park South in New York, he told Losey: "I can't deny that I feel intimidated but nevertheless it remains very exciting and a good deal of what I gleaned from your notes was exciting. But Jesus! What a task! I must remind you that I'm not as young as I used to be. If you have any further observations, don't hesitate to send them to me!!!!!!"[11] By December he had finished the draft. Some years later, Pinter would explain the nature of his fruitful partnership with Losey: "although the hand which actually does the writing is my own, I consider these works [*Accident* and *The Go-Between*] as written with Mr Losey. Our two minds are responsible for them".[12] Losey sent Pinter a new batch of notes on the latest draft, one of them suggesting that Hartley himself should play Leo Colston as an old man and do the narration.

On December 15, contracts had finally been signed bringing the dispute with Velaise to an end. Hartley recorded gleefully: "The room where this took place, 72 Brook Street [headquarters of Heyman's company, World Film Services], was so splendiferous it was like Cleopatra's barge and beggared all description. Even the cigarette boxes seemed to open by electricity or magic – though I don't suppose they did. The rest of the company was very abstemious, but I had two strong dry martinis to celebrate the occasion".[13] Filled with a new enthusiasm, Hartley suggested budding young actresses he knew for the part of Marian, and a young musician he had met from Tennessee, Kenton Coe, as a possible composer for the music. Losey sent Bernard Delfont, Lew Grade's brother and head of EMI, a copy of Pinter's new screenplay, adding that "it would be marvellous if we could all combine to make another Grade/Pinter/Losey classic – which will also make money. Good reading".[14]

At the beginning of February, 1969 Losey and his long-standing English girlfriend Patricia headed for Norfolk. Patricia was no stranger to the region as her father had been rector of Ludham, to the east of Norwich, in the 1930s. Later in the 1970s Losey wrote about his first impressions of the county for an anthology on East Anglia edited by Angus Wilson. He was impressed by the pine forests of Thetford Chase, which reminded him of Dartmouth, his old Ivy League college in New Hampshire. Losey and Patricia visited Bradenham Hall, which Hartley had described as a plain red brick Georgian box. But they found that the house had been extensively remodelled in the middle of the twentieth century and its picturesque appearance no longer had the grandeur implied in Hartley's description. On his return, Losey asked his friend Baroness Moura Budberg for advice. A flamboyant figure then in her late seventies, Budberg was a Russian aristocrat who, after the Revolution, had been the mistress of both Maxim Gorky and H.G. Wells and was generally thought to have been a double-agent for Russia and MI5. In recent years she had written screenplays: her adaptation of Chekhov's *The Sea Gull* was directed by Sidney Lumet in 1968 and she often advised Losey on scripts. She suggested consulting Sir John Betjeman, and Losey wrote to Hartley for an introduction. Hartley responded by suggesting that Losey contact another friend of his, the architectural historian James Lees-Milne, who had been Historic Buildings Adviser to the National Trust.

Lees-Milne wrote back enthusiastically and suggested eleven houses including Wolterton, Aylsham Old Hall, Stanhoe, Barton, Cranmer and Shotesham, all in Norfolk. He also suggested the Moot House, Wiltshire, Nether Lypiatt near Wotten-under-Edge, Tintinhull, Buscot Rectory and his own family house, Alderley Grange, in Gloucestershire, adding "would that Alderley were in Norfolk". But Losey was coming to the conclusion that the house, and indeed all the film's shooting, were going to have to be in Norfolk. In that case, suggested Lees-Milne, he could recommend two old friends of his in Norfolk who could offer first-hand advice: they were Robert Ketton-Cremer, squire of Felbrigg Hall near Cromer, and Wilhelmine Harrod, wife of the Oxford economist Sir Roy Harrod and known as Billa, who lived in the Old Rectory at Holt. Ketton-Cremer, however, was ailing (he would die in December, 1969) and unable to help, but Billa Harrod, who had been the co-author of the ever-popular *Shell Guide to Norfolk* and was active in the Campaign for the Protection of Rural England, leapt at the chance to share her knowledge of the county.

Suddenly, in April, 1969, Delfont pulled out. On April 20, Hartley wrote to Losey: "So my prophetic soul was right! ... *The Go-Between*, which has been a blessing in so many ways, has been rather a curse in others. I hope that Leo hasn't put one of his curses on it!"[15] Hartley suggested hopefully that a legacy he had recently received could perhaps enable him to finance the film himself. Losey reponded: "[N]o one can inherit enough" these days to pay for a film, but went on to report that Delfont had changed his mind: "*The Go-Between* has now been set up for next year. Why it was possible to set it up for next year with the same people and not this I shall never be able to explain to myself or anyone else ... Anyway, I am to begin work on April 1st next year; shooting to commence on July 1st, 1970. What will probably happen now is that we will have a divine summer in 1969 and nothing but rain in 1970. But never mind – we shall manage ... if you were a vulgar man I would treat you to a fine set of obscene expletives on the situation".[16]

The explanation was that Bryan Forbes, matinee star turned screenwriter and director, who had been hired by Delfont to run Associated British Pictures (which had just been bought by EMI), had persuaded Delfont to change his mind. Forbes's brief was to revitalize the British film industry with "quality" productions, and Forbes declared that Pinter's screenplay was "sheer joy".[17] He told the *Guardian* that *The Go-Between* was "Perhaps the best film script I have ever seen in my life".[18]

Losey took on a pot-boiler for the summer of 1969, Robert Shaw's *Figures in a Landscape*, and after returning from the shoot in Spain in September, resumed his work finding locations. In November he wrote to John Heyman: "I am quite concerned that the area in which we should work should be Norfolk, around Norwich.

Melton Constable Hall, Norfolk, circa 1970. Built in the 1660s by Sir Jacob Astley, it is one of the earliest examples of a classical country house in England. Sold by Astley's descendants in the 1950s, the empty house was owned by a local farmer, Geoffrey Harrold, who rented it to the production company as a location for The Go-Between.

It is an area unexplored, unseen, with a much more interesting countryside than the South, free from modern encroachment. The light is better, although nothing much in the script connects it specifically with this area".[19]

The post of art director had still not been filled. Losey told Hartley he was hoping to get Jocelyn Herbert, the influential stage designer at the National Theatre.[20] Herbert had done some film work, most notably for Tony Richardson's *Tom Jones* (1963) and for Lindsay Anderson's *If* (1968), but her work was impressionistic rather than realistic. Losey's friend and agent Robin Fox suggested Carmen Dillon, who was as different as could be from either Richard MacDonald or Jocelyn Herbert. Described by many as "a formidable presence" on the set, Dillon was one of three unmarried sisters – the other two were a hospital matron and the founder of Dillon's University Bookshop respectively – who shared a large Edwardian flat off Kensington Church Street. Carmen Dillon once remarked that her job allowed no time for marriage. A veteran of the studio system, she had worked for Anthony "Puffin" Asquith on a number of his films in the 1940s and 50s,[21] and had been the first woman art director in British cinema, making her name with such classics as *Robin Hood* and *Henry V*. By 1969 she was sixty-one years old and could rely on first-hand experience of many of the settings and social conventions in Hartley's book. Her grounding in the studio system, however, made her reluctant to embrace location shooting with much enthusiasm. But Losey was determined, writing to Dillon: "I am very insistent on shooting the entire picture on location with an independent crew – both interior and exterior redressing, redecorating, rebuilding as necessary, all of which will take some doing as we will be operating on a somewhat restricted budget".

Lord and Lady Walpole were receptive to the idea of renting out Wolterton, a Palladian house some twelve miles north of Norwich, but the house would have had to be completely emptied, decorated and then refurnished. A more likely candidate proved to be Hanworth Hall, owned by Michael Barclay of the Norfolk banking family, which dated from the end of the seventeenth century. But the problems of moving a family's accumulated possessions of seventy years were daunting.

Quite by chance, Dillon heard of an empty Carolean house about fifteen miles from Norwich. Melton Constable Hall had been the seat of the Astley family, Lords Hastings, and stood in the middle of an estate owned by them since the thirteenth century. They had sold the house and about half of the land to the Duke of Westminster in the 1950s; subsequently the house itself had been tenanted but in 1956 the estate had been bought by a local farmer, Geoffrey Harrold, who had extensive holdings in the area. In the post-war era of intensive farming, Harrold had brought economies of scale to the operation of the farm, but he had no use for the mansion, which was left empty. Curiously, neither Billa Harrod or James Lees-Milne had suggested Melton, although Lees-Milne had visited the house in 1942 at the request of Lord Hastings, who had been considering giving it to the National Trust. How Carmen Dillon heard about the empty house remains a mystery, but in January 1970 she was negotiating with Harrold, who was quite amenable to rent out the house and its grounds for the summer. The fee would be £1,500.

In the meantime, Dillon agreed with Barclay that they would shoot the scenes of Ted Burgess's house and farmyard on the estate at Hanworth. She also negotiated to rent a field adjoining the farmyard which Barclay agreed to have sown with wheat which could be harvested the following August by Ted using an authentic cutter.

Melton Constable made shooting entirely on location a reality. Large pictures which still belonged to the Astley family hung on the stairs, but otherwise the rooms were devoid of furniture and could be dressed by Dillon as

A detail from a water-colour sketch by Carmen Dillon of the arrangement of the "Smoking-Room" at Melton Constable Hall, used for a scene with Lord Trimingham, Mr Maudsley and the boy Leo.

an authentic late Victorian country house. "The gardens have gone" she noted, "although they are said to be tidied up in the summer; it looks as if the lawns have gone, although it was hard to judge through the snow … [inside] everything has to be decorated and furnished. But I think this applies to any house we find, unless we can find very old people living as they used to do".[22]

Losey alerted the crew whom he had put on notice that he was to do *The Go-Between* in the summer of 1969 and informed them that the production was postponed until the following year. Now once again he set about gathering together his favourite team, which would be a mixture of freelancers and regular staff on the payroll of Associated British.

Jerry Fisher, who had worked for Losey on *Accident* and *Secret Ceremony*, was the obvious choice for cinematographer. Pamela Davies, his continuity girl who had worked for him since 1957, accepted with alacrity. For costumes, Carmen Dillon had found John Furniss, noting that he was very good at men's clothes, "which are *very* difficult for this period. The women's are beautifully easy to wear, particularly summer clothes, but the slight differences between Trimingham and the tiny bit less U are very subtle if they are not to look jokey. And Ted's are the most difficult". In the event, having laid the groundwork for the "feel" of the costumes, Furniss was unable to come on location, having been hired for *Nicholas and Alexandra*, and his assistant Camilla Farmer assumed the role. "I was completely green," Farmer remembers.[23]

Losey had approached Julie Christie for the role of eighteen-year-old Marian several years before. Now, he was tempted to consider using unknowns for the roles of the two lovers, but this proved unpopular with Delfont and EMI. Among the stars considered were Mia Farrow, star of *Secret Ceremony* (she refused, being pregnant with

The west front of Melton Constable Hall as the scaffolding rises. Ultimately the seventy-foot tower would enable a single shot to travel from figures on the lawn up to the window of Leo and Marcus's second-floor bedroom. Some of the neo-classical stone urns on the balustrade were in poor condition and would have to be replaced with plaster replicas.

twins), Marianne Faithful, Sarah Miles, Lynn Redgrave and Judy Huxtable, the wife of Peter Cook. In the lists drawn up under "no names" there are Charlotte Rampling and Nicola Paget. For the part of Ted Burgess, we find David Warner, Albert Finney and Tom Courtney listed. Mick Jagger was added to one list with a question mark. Among the "no names" were Ian McShane, John Stride and Michael Billington. In June 1970 Losey would write to Billington explaining that they could not give him the part because of the "name" requirements. Delfont had won that point.

Margaret Leighton and Edward Fox playing cricket outside the west front of Melton Constable Hall. Despite repeated mowing, the neglected lawns were bald and had to be painted green.

The supporting roles were to go to stalwart professionals. For the part of Mrs Maudsley, Maggie Smith, Vivien Merchant (Pinter's wife), Joan Greenwood, Margaret Tyzack and Deborah Kerr were all considered. Kerr was insulted when Losey failed to telephone her at an appointed time. Also considered at a late stage was Diana Dors, as well as Wendy Craig, who had been in *The Servant* but was not highly regarded by Losey. The final choice, Margaret Leighton, would turn out to be an inspired one; she would add so much smouldering intensity to her part that it would win her a British Academy Award. For Mr Maudsley, Michael Gough, a commanding presence in film and theatre for the previous twenty years, was an immediate choice, as was Michael Redgrave for the role of the older Leo. Lord Trimingham was also comparatively easy to cast, with Edward Fox the obvious

Michael Redgrave as the older Leo Colston in the present-day scenes of the film.

Left to right: Simon Hume-Kendall (Denys), Dominic Guard (Leo), Richard Gibson (Marcus) and Raewyn Saxon, their chaperone, outside Melton Constable Hall. Simon and Richard were sixth-formers at Radley and had had no acting experience; Dominic came from an acting family and had appeared in a play at the National Theatre.

candidate. He was the son of Robin Fox and elder brother of James Fox, who had starred in *The Servant*. Others considered but rejected early on were Edward Woodward, David Warner and, curiously, Peter Cook, the satirist, not a natural actor but nevertheless considered a bankable name. Among the "unknowns" listed were James Villiers, Jeremy Brett and John Standing.

Casting the boys proved to be more difficult. Losey's own son Joshua was considered, but Losey later explained to him that he could not give him the part lest he be accused of nepotism. Harold Pinter's son, Daniel, was also considered, as were the two sons of Ros Chatto (who was to become Losey's agent after Robin Fox died) and Brian Rix's son. Nigel Havers auditioned for the part of Denys and was declared "very good" but did not get the part. Finally, two inexperienced sixth-formers at Radley, Richard Gibson and Simon Hume-Kendall, were chosen, and the agent Boaty Boatwright wrote to the union Equity requesting that they be allowed to play the roles of the two Maudsley brothers: "[I]t is essential to have authentic upper class accents of 1900", she explained.

For Leo himself, however, it was clear that Dominic Guard was the ideal candidate early on in his audition with Losey and Pinter. The son of acting parents, Guard had already appeared on stage at the National Theatre. What Losey and the others did not know though was that the boy had a stammer, which would only become apparent after shooting began. In the scene with Mr Maudsley and Lord Trimingham in the Smoking-Room, in take after take Guard sucked in air. He later admitted to Losey and Patricia that he had been taught to do so as an antidote to his stammer.

With all the other roles cast, those of Marian and Ted remained a problem. Delfont, responding no doubt to calls from Hollywood (MGM had been sold fifty per cent of the production as part of a cooperative deal between Associated British and the American studio), announced that Julie Christie and Alan Bates, who had just starred in *Far from the Madding Crowd*, were necessary to secure the investment. Losey had doubts whether Christie, now twenty-nine, could still play the eighteen-year-old Marian. Christie agreed. Not only that, but could she also play the role of old Marian towards the end of the film? Jerry Fisher was quizzed about both roles: could he make Christie look both eighteen and seventy? "If you give me carte blanche so that each shot of her is entirely controlled to that purpose, it's conceivable ... But if you think I can make Julie Christie appear eighteen and others look the age they are, with her taking tea round to people sitting at tables on the lawn on a summer's day, then no", he said. In the end, Fisher remembers, "Joe was told, if you get Julie Christie and Alan Bates, you will get the money".[24]

Bates was not a problem, but Julie Christie had not made a film for two years and was reclusive. The ups and down of her affair with the American heart-throb Warren Beatty had been dissected by the popular press on both sides of the Atlantic and it had left her wary of any publicity. Her response was non-committal; Beatty entered into the negotiations on her behalf. By mid-May, 1970, with less than six weeks to go before filming was to begin, still no deal had been reached and in desperation Losey cabled Beatty at Delmonico's in New York: "Have no wish to interfere with money matters and negotiations but would appreciate your giving definitive answer today to John Heyman as the project otherwise has no more than a day's life in it. Stop. It would be a great pity for so many people's work and hopes to disappear simply through default. Losey". It was not to be until June 10 that Christie's participation was confirmed. She was to receive $50,000 plus an equal share with Losey and Bates of ten per cent of EMI's gross receipts above the cost of production. Her fee and Pinter's, of $75,000 plus five per cent of the revenue, were stratospheric compared to the other fees. Losey himself was to get a mere £17,500 plus £2,500 expenses and his cut of the profits; Leighton a flat fee of £2,500, Edward Fox £1,750. The total budget was just over £500,000.[25]

Shortly before filming began, Losey sent the main cast members a memorandum marked "Confidential" that outlined his thoughts on the atmosphere of the film, and the main characters:

> THE STORY
> On one level the story is simply as told, but on other but more difficult levels, it is –
>
> The story of the destruction of a little boy by the unthinking, but not necessarily malicious, use of him by a variety of adults, propelled by their self-interest and passions. The boy is on the edge of innocence, but not entirely innocent. In other words, he is caught at a time of delicate balance. Among the characters, only Maudsley is totally aware of the little boy and his problems. At the very end, some glimpse of what it means to the child comes to Marian momentarily and to Ted perhaps more deeply.
> I am interested and concerned with showing the span of a whole life in a setting which changes in seventy years not so very much, and in the dead-end of Norfolk the changes consist mainly of telephone wires, power pylons, television aerials etc. I am speaking only about the purely environmental things, not the machines etc. One of the accomplishments of this extraordinary script is that in the most economical and precise way it encompasses a whole life-span and shows that one person's life-span is hardly a dot in time. This, I think, interacts with point one to heighten the tragedy of a potentially good life destroyed or blighted. The script, by its scrambling of time, i.e. putting contemporary dialogue over 1900 and vice versa; telling the Colston story non-chronologically; sometimes mixing both past

and present should make it possible to convey at least emotionally, something of what is meant by the time continuum curve, the coexistence of past, present and future, given finiteness only by the need of human beings to break it down into arbitrary time units ... anyway, this is the aspiration.

He goes on to outline the characters – "Marian, beautiful, wilful, spoilt, rebellious, wasted, because really in a reasonable society she could be quite a useful human being" ... "Ted is a passion, but the passion becomes almost an obsession because it is the symbol of rebellion against everything".[26]

Alan Bates was delighted: "[N]o director had ever done that before," he remarked. The groundwork had been done and the scene set for a summer of happy creativity in Norfolk.

1 Hartley interview, *Guardian*, March 16, 1971; Kulik, p. 331.
2 Taylor, p. 202.
3 JWL/1/18/11; Caute, p. 254.
4 Quoted in J.W. Lambert's obituary of Hartley, *Sunday Times*, December 17, 1972.
5 De Rham, p. 234.
6 JWL/1/18/11.
7 Caute, p. 7.
8 Billington, *Pinter*, p. 206.
9 As Pinter's biographer Michael Billington observes: "[T]he fact is that in our emotional lives the present is constantly shaped and informed by the past"; ibid.
10 Hartley to Losey, August 15, 1968, JWL/1/18/11; Hartley's letter to his mother is in the possession of his trustees, and I am very grateful to David Riddington for making it available to me.
11 Pinter to Losey, September 4, 1968, JWL/1/18/11.
12 Pinter, letter to *The Times*, October 19, 1972.
13 Hartley to Losey, December 15, 1968, JWL/1/18/11.
14 Losey to Delfont, February 6, 1969, JWL/1/18/11.
15 Ibid.
16 Ibid.
17 Forbes, p. 234.
18 *Guardian*, August 9, 1969.
19 Losey to Heyman, November 24, 1969, JWL/1/18/18.
20 Losey to Hartley, February 25, 1969, JWL/1/18/13.
21 Minney, pp. 241, 249, 252-4.
22 Carmen Dillon, location notes, n.d., JWL/1/18/13.
23 Camilla Farmer interview with CH, August 5, 2011.
24 Hayward, p. 108.
25 JWL/1/18/13.
26 I am grateful to Terry Hodgkinson for giving me a copy of this memorandum.

Julie Christie on her bicycle at Melton Constable Hall.

3 Norfolk Idyll

AT THE START, FILMING *THE GO-BETWEEN* was far from idyllic. A few days before cast and crew met at Melton Constable Hall in Norfolk, Losey and Heyman were still unsure whether the money would be in place in time for Chris Chrisafis, the payroll clerk who would go on to be a highly successful film producer himself, to pay the first week's wages. Nonetheless, the cast and crew showed up, coming by train, using the first-class rail vouchers enclosed with their joining instructions, or by car. "It says something about the commitment everyone already felt towards the project," observes Edward Fox. Some checked into the hotels assigned to them by the company: Margaret Leighton, Julie Christie and other cast members at the faded magnificence of the Hotel de Paris in Cromer, others at pubs in Holt and Fakenham, or in bed-and-breakfast places. The three boys, together with their New Zealander chaperone, Raewyn Saxon, were in a boarding house close to Melton Constable. In time, it would prove inadequate and they too checked into the Hotel de Paris. The amusement arcades on Cromer Pier proved an irresistible attraction for them and they begged small change from the crew whenever they could.

Margaret Leighton, Edward Fox and Michael Gough relax between takes on Heydon village green.

Julie Christie, Edward Fox and others soon found local cottages to rent. Christie rented Burgh Hall near Aylsham, while Fox took a small house overlooking the marshes at Cley-next-the-Sea, as did Michael and Anneke Gough with two small children in tow, and Terry Hodgkinson, the 2nd assistant director. Alan Bates installed his wife Vicky and their baby at Bale Hall about three miles from Melton. Losey's girlfriend Patricia had found a converted barn – a rarity in Norfolk in 1970 – at the end of a track looking towards the sea at Brancaster. It meant an hour's drive to the set every morning, but it was worth it, as it provided a place for quiet work well away from the cast and crew, and there were plenty of rooms for guests such as Harold Pinter, Moura Budberg or Losey's son Joshua. On occasion Dominic Guard would come to stay the weekend (he and Joshua were the same age).

"I almost felt I was living the life" *Roger Lloyd Pack*

Patricia set about housekeeping and starting a vegetable garden. By the end of the summer, Marsh Barn had proved its worth as a peaceful haven for Losey. He could retreat there in the evenings and prepare his notes for the next day's shooting, for Losey was a meticulous planner, and practised what had been described as "pre-design".[1] Each day on the set he knew Pinter's screenplay so well that he seldom had to refer to Pamela Davies, the continuity girl, to remind him of a line or a set-up.[2]

Losey was conscious that time was limited and money was going to be tight. And the weather looked uncertain. Yet he wrote in jubilant tone to Hartley on July 13, "We are actually finally beginning the shooting today with an excellent crew and cast and splendid locations. All that we lack is time, money, weather guarantees and understanding from the commercial side as ever ... I see that there is a small place called Trimingham which can't be more than thirty miles away from your original house. I haven't had time to find out whether there are viscounts entombed in the church. Are there? And shall I use it, or shall we be sued for libel?"[3] Billa Harrod invited Hartley to come and stay with her at Holt Rectory and watch some of the filming. Hartley promised to come but kept putting it off until it was too late and filming was over.

The luxury of space at Melton Constable Hall was appreciated by everyone. As Losey afterwards recalled: "Melton Court *was* the film, the home of the film. Here Michael Gough slowly matured the part of Mr Maudsley until he *was* Mr Maudsley. Here Edward Fox grew into the Viscount, and Fox and Gough began to converse with each other and behave as though they were in fact the people out of Hartley by Harold Pinter. Here Julie Christie could be glimpsed through the cornfields riding her bicycle in costume or jeans, wandering the paths with her thoughts, alone. Or were they Miss Maudsley's thoughts? Here, on the lawns, the magnificent Margaret Leighton with all of her period stays and her sad crippling rheumatism, and perhaps the beginnings of the disease that took her from us, played cricket in costume with the crew. And here the boy Dominic Guard, struggled with his

Extras playing house guests, on the steps of the west front of Melton Constable Hall; left to right are Jane Clarke, Lizzie Harvey, Susan Bradley, Miriam Rawlinson and Veronica Bedford.

shyness in the leading role and slept off his exhaustion in the huge upstairs living-room which was my study for the duration".[4]

The leading cast members were able to have their own dressing rooms (Margaret Leighton's was palatial), and other rooms were given over to offices, a projection room, make-up and hairdressing, wardrobe, carpentry and a canteen. The food was prepared by Mr Cook, the caterer, in his bus parked alongside the hall. The rooms in the house which were to be used as sets had been furnished using a combination of hired props and locally bought items. A night watchman with Alsatian was employed to guard the house. The dog refused to go into one of the upstairs rooms, giving rise to ghost stories until it was discovered that the animal was avoiding the acid fumes that rose through the floorboards from the batteries used for the camera equipment in the room below.

Melton's many stables, carriage houses (one of which retained its nineteenth-century horse-drawn fire engine) and outhouses provided space for workshops and storage. John Bailey, a young man taken on by the crew as a general helper, years later recalled a chance encounter with Julie Christie outside one of these outhouses: "I was trudging through the outhouses sweating under buckets of rubble, the grime and plaster of centuries in my hair when a young woman of fabulous beauty appeared out of a doorway. She wore Edwardian dress and a bonnet and looked at me directly with eyes bluer than the sky and smiled a smile that can turn me to jelly still when I remember it. 'Hello', she said. 'It's too hot for work, isn't it?' I tried and tried as the seconds raced but I could say nothing in reply, words just sticking in my throat. I forced myself to return her smile but my face was frozen and I must have looked like a strangulated ape".[5]

Although empty, Melton still had a resident housekeeper, Phyllis Youngman, and Jack Carter, the agent for the estate, also lived there. Each evening, when he prepared the next day's call sheets, Terry Hodgkinson got into the habit of asking Carter about the weather prospects and every time was given an uncannily accurate forecast. "How do you country people do it?" asked an incredulous Spike Priggen. "I watch Anglia Television every night," replied Carter.

Stephanie Kaye, the head hairdresser, together with her assistant Gladys Leakey, Gladys's husband, Phil, who was a make-up artiste, and Bob Lawrence, in charge of make-up, had rented a cottage called Prospect House at Hindolveston and they would travel together the two miles to Melton every morning. Stephanie modelled Julie Christie's hair on the portraits of girls by the American turn-of-the-century artist Charles Gibson Dana known as Gibson Girls. It was a complicated arrangement that involved three sections: the front and back were the actress's own, but the middle section was false. Stephanie also did Dominic Guard's and Alan Bates's hair; Phil did Margaret Leighton's.[6] Bob Lawrence experimented with the scar that disfigures Viscount Trimingham's face. Hartley's book called for it to pull his eye down "exposing a tract of glistening red under-lid" but in the end, with a glance at the box office, the scar became more like a duelling scar than a horrific disfigurement.

Carmen Dillon had arrived with two assistants, Tessa Davies, who was in charge of the sets, and Martin Gascoigne. Peter Hammond, eighteen-year-old son of the manager of Barclay's Bank in Holt, was also taken on as a "gofer" by Dillon, who put him in sole charge of her aged yellow Labrador, Andy. Peter was between

Julia Hull (née Howlett) with two extras during the cricket match scene at Thornage Common.

school and university and relished the thought of working on a film for the summer, although some of the tasks he was asked to do were bizarre: could he find a rain gauge by the following morning? Two live rabbits by mid-afternoon? A cooked ham? Tom Bishop, who ran a business selling bygones in a barn at Aylsham, was a good source for many of the more obscure props needed, as was Patrick Townsend, "The Mad Hatter" of Weybourne. Townsend had been a broker on the Baltic Exchange and now ran an antique shop on the coast. He was frequently seen wearing eighteenth-century dress.

The biggest problem was to be the deadly nightshade (*Atropa belladonna*) that plays such a prominent part in the film. None could be found in the immediate vicinity of Melton Constable, and an appeal was broadcast on the local television stations. Dick Bagnall-Oakley, a television naturalist who lived nearby, confided to Peter Hammond that a large clump of it was growing at Horsey Mere some fifteen miles away. Peter came back with several dust bins full of it. By the time they came to film it supposedly growing in one of the outhouses beside the hall, it was decidedly wilted, and certainly did not look as if it "tipped the roofless walls" or that "it pressed into their crannies, groping for an outlet". Even with the addition of some fake berries hastily made by Dillon and her crew, it was not convincing. Still not satisfied with the way it looked in the rushes, after the shoot was finished, Dillon would create a much more convincing fake deadly nightshade plant in the studios and shots of it would be added to the final cut.

Filming on location in a house, even if empty, presented a host of problems that Jerry Fisher, the cinematographer, and Carmen Dillon strove to surmount. Losey described the house as "not beautiful" to an Anglia Television reporter, but went on to say that it was "better than any studio we could possibly hope for or get".[7] Dillon felt otherwise: filming on location, she explained to John Russell Taylor, could make real things look artificial. "Look out of that window and what you see couldn't look more like a painted backdrop. If it was a backdrop, everyone would be self-conscious about it, but since we know it's real, we take it on trust that it will also look real".[8] For Fisher, the filters he had to place over the windows caused endless problems of lighting, and the weather could interfere with a scene even indoors.

Outdoors, when the sun did come out, it was a different matter. The corn had ripened in their rented field at Hanworth and at the first bit of sunshine the crew raced over to film Ted Burgess as he harvested it. Horses pulled a real sail cutter from the 1870s belonging to Teddy Mack of Pond Farm, Bodham.

Susan Howard (left), who had driven her mother's trap, pulled by their pony Apache, over from Norwich for the church scene at Heydon.

Associated British Productions lorry with the Holkham carriage.

The script required a number of carts and carriages, and driving horses and ponies as well as some farm horses. Local enthusiasts such as Julia Howlett, Mrs Bell and Elizabeth Howard provided them; others were supplied by George Mossman's firm. When they filmed the church scenes at Heydon and the cricket match at Thornage, Dr Howard, who was a vet in Norwich, sent her daughter, Susan, in her trap pulled by her pony Apache. For some of the carriage scenes, Terry Hodgkinson's Citroën 2CV, its hatchback removed, was enlisted as a camera dolly. Once during filming, an open landau, with Mr and Mrs Maudsley and others inside, was shot trotting through the ford at Thornage; the party were on their way to the picnic. Losey said to the coachman: "Do it again but have the horses gallop through the water so there's a big splash". The coachman, who had worked as a real one in his youth, replied: "If I had cantered these horses through a ford with my employer in the back, I would have been fired on the spot". Losey cancelled the re-shoot.

Losey would be the first to admit that he was no countryman. He wrote a memorandum to the sound engineer Peter Hanford, the dubbing editor Garth Craven and the editor Reginald Beck: "In the smoking scene [one of the first scenes to be filmed, with Leo, Trimingham and Mr Maudsley] somewhere near the end I think it would be dramatic and useful to have the sound of distant rifle fire – late evening hunting".[10]

Mostly to shield Julie Christie from being hounded by paparazzi, who were eager to photograph her and Warren Beatty in the lush landscape of Norfolk and ask them when they were going to wed, John Heyman instituted a "closed set" policy for the first ten days of shooting. After that, all journalists admitted would have to be vetted, but no interviews were to be allowed with Christie. She finally relented for Anglia Television in late August.[11] Christie did also break her rule of silence to speak to the local press about her visit to a local intensive pig farm: "It was so appalling", she said, "I couldn't believe that that was what was meant by 'factory farming'. Animals were being kept in a concentration camp".[12] Warren Beatty announced that he would become a vegetarian, like Alan Bates and his wife.

Word got out, through television, the local newspapers and word of mouth, that work, as extras or helpers, would be available at Melton. Auditions for extras were held at Holt, Blakeney and in Norwich. Fourteen-year-old Stephen Fry, then going through teenage angst at his parents' house in nearby Bootle, heeded the call and bicycled over to Melton to offer his services. They were rejected and he rode home again.[13] John Ritchie, who had just retired as the butler at Felbrigg Hall near Cromer, was engaged to play the Maudsleys' butler. He would also provide useful advice on laying the dining table and on matters of etiquette. Each of the actors had to have a stand-in, recruited from the locals. Leo's stand-in was Richard Mann, sixteen years of age, who lived in Fakenham and worked in J.W. Powell's saddler's shop in Oak Street, Fakenham.

Shooting began on July 13 with one of the most technically difficult shots in the film: that of the two boys coming down the grand staircase. The camera operator was strapped to a boom in order to use a hand-held camera. Then outside to film a scene on the terrace with Julie Christie, who appeared from make-up and rushed up to Steve Smith, the clapper/loader, and, much to the surprise of the rest of the crew, hugged and kissed him – they had worked together on Julie's last film. On a shoot, the crew are there every day, and they see everything and everyone, while actors come and go. The dog in the scene is introduced to Leo as Dry Toast and for the rest of the shoot Gerry Fisher would refer to Smith as Dry Toast.

Harold Pinter's fascination with words drove him to ring the office in the evening from time to time as Terry Hodgkinson was preparing the next day's Call Sheets. "What phrases are they using?" he would ask Terry, for the crew would take lines from the script and use them as catch phrases: "Shall you be going to Goodwood?" "Shall we make up a party to go to Norwich?"

Another difficult shot involved building a seventy-foot tower of scaffolding up the side of the house. As Losey later described it: "It's evening, the camera swoops down towards the couple on the lawn; then there's a high angle shot up to the top of the house, where the two children are in bed. This was very important, because what was happening down below, the singing and the dancing, the laughter, the elegance was part of the consciousness of the little boy in bed with his sleeping friend. I doubt whether even technicians would realize there was a zoom there".[14] Steve Smith remembers how very difficult a shot it was, and frightening, too. "Mike Rutter [the focus puller] was physically sick when he looked down," he remembers.[15]

John Heyman arrived with gifts for the leading cast members and also for Carmen Dillon. That evening Harold Pinter arrived to stay with the Loseys. The next day they shot the scene of the dinner that follows young Leo's arrival: "There are curses and curses, you see". The food spread on the dining table was real, and had to be left for several days afterwards in case any re-shoots or detail shots were needed. Meanwhile, Pinter, Patricia and the author Penelope Mortimer (who was preparing to write a book about the making of the film, a project that would be abandoned) went to see Billa Harrod at Holt Rectory. She had been asked for advice about the scene of family prayers and had in turn consulted her sister, her mother and her friend Lady Hastings, who had come to Melton as a bride in 1907. Lady Harrod's son Dominick, who was also present, remembers that they chose the correct collect for a day in late July, and decided that everyone would have knelt facing their chairs.[16] On returning to Melton Constable Hall, Pinter related what they had been told to Losey and Carmen Dillon.

The following Monday, they shot the scene. When the set had been arranged, Rex Hobbs, the props man, produced half a dozen late Victorian prayer books, garnered from local antique shops. Losey chose a plain black one for Mr Maudsley to use. "Why did you chose the plainest one?" asked Terry Hodgkinson. "Because it won't detract from the action," explained Losey.[17] Years later, Hodgkinson would remember, as a twenty-eight-year-old 2nd assistant director, being encouraged by Losey to ask him questions: "It was rather like an advanced hands-on film course, although I didn't realise it at the time. We never do".[18] Patricia had had lunch with Lady Silvia Combe, sister of the Earl of Leicester, and afterwards she brought her back to Melton to watch the shooting. "We were able to watch from the stairs as the camera was at the bottom … Joe asked Michael Gough to read Hartley's description of the scene from the book. At the end, Joe said, very quietly, 'That's the atmosphere' and then they rehearsed".[19]

Losey's quiet approach with actors was respected by them. That summer, Margaret Leighton referred to Losey as the best director she had worked with.[20] Roger Lloyd Pack recalls Losey as "completely self-effacing on the set – I admired that; he didn't need to exert himself".[21] Edward Fox remembers "he had a liking for actors". He described to his mother how Losey directed: "He does nothing. The fact is that he's there, and he looks at you, and you catch his eye, and you know what he wants. And then he uses the camera in such a way that he gives you a chance to portray whatever it is almost by telepathy: what he's conveyed to you and knows you can do. He concentrates so hard. Once … a one-shot scene, which he did in one take, he was so absorbed in what he was doing, as was I, that, as he was pulling the camera back – and we were both in a sort of hypnotic trance, not saying anything at all – going back and back, he was nearly bloody killed by this huge camera squashing him against the wall. This was the way he held his actors, with his mind, and doing scenes in one take …"[22] In one scene, Marian opened a letter from Ted and after reading it she automatically put it back in the envelope. "Just drop it where you like," said Losey, "that's what servants are for" – just as Marcus tells Leo to do with his clothes in one of the first scenes of the film.[23]

But Losey still had to build an effective working relationship with Julie Christie. One Monday, she arrived late on set, having been invited on Sam Spiegel's yacht for the weekend. Losey, who was normally quiet and sensitive in his approach with actors, blew up in a rage: "I would accept that from a star like Elizabeth Taylor, but not from you!" he bellowed.[24] Years later, Jerry Fisher suggested: "It's quite possible he said it to achieve a certain effect. Joe was nervous, too, and against anything that exhibited a disrespect to the pressure that we were under to realize the film".[25] Later, after the shoot, Losey and Christie would exchange pleasant letters speaking of their "non-communication".

Christie had been reluctant to return to films after *Petulia* two years before. Warren Beatty had convinced her to take the role in *The Go-Between*. But she enjoyed being in the countryside, where she could ride her bicycle, or practise driving (she was about to take her driving test) in an old Saab. She confided to Julia Howlett one day, as she was being made up, how she envied Julia's free lifestyle and life in the country.[26]

The heavy rain and wind continued. They were running out of interior shots to film – even in interiors shots the bad weather could be seen through a window. The tension was growing. But nonetheless everyone felt that they were involved in the creation of a great film. Jerry Fisher had come to dinner at Marsh Barn and declared that if he were to die that day and *The Go-Between* were his last picture, he would be satisfied. "Several people have made the same sort of statement," Patricia noted laconically in her diary.[27]

The scene in the kitchen. Left to right: Dominic Guard (Leo), Geraldine Bird (2nd cook), Joan Harrison (cook).

On the following Tuesday, plans to shoot the tea party on the terrace were relinquished because of the weather. Instead they shot the scene where Leo runs into the kitchen and is given the mixing bowl to lick by one of the cooks. Joan Harrison of Wiveton and Geraldine Bird of Briningham had been chosen as the two cooks at an audition at the Feathers in Holt the previous week. Geraldine remembers, "A man told me to pour the batter

Filming the tea party at Melton Constable Hall. Left to right: Peter Wood (camera grip), unidentified, Steve Smith (clapper/loader), Dudley Lovell (camera operator), Gerry Gavigan (3rd assistant director), unidentified, Jerry Fisher (cinematographer), Pamela Davies, unidentified.

out of the pan into the bowl and give the bowl to the boy. I said: 'Shouldn't it be the other way around? Shouldn't I pour the batter out of the bowl into the pan and then give him the bowl?' The man thought for a moment and then said, 'Yes you're right – do it that way'. Afterwards someone asked me if I had known who I was speaking to – it was the great director Joseph Losey! I would never have dared to open my mouth if I had known!"

They were finally able to film the picnic scenes, and other exterior shots, on Tuesday, July 28, although the weather was still unpredictable. The first sunny day was Thursday, July 30 and they used it to film the scene of Marian being read to in her hammock and other garden scenes where Trimingham (Edward Fox) enlists Leo's help as "Mercury". "Edward was brilliant," noted Patricia.[28] It would be his performance in *The Go-Between* that would land Fox his celebrated role in Fred Zinneman's 1973 film *The Day of the Jackal*.[29] The areas of lawn around the hall had been so neglected that repeated mowing had merely reduced them to expanses of earth. In desperation they sprayed the ground with green paint, which came off onto the female extras' long dresses as they walked across it.

Losey sent a guarded progress report to the producers: "In sixteen days of shooting we have had two half-days of partial sun, one full day of intermittent sun, and today (July 30) the first day of consistent sun." He recorded that on that day it had taken nineteen set-ups to do five-and-a-half pages of screenplay totalling approximately four minutes of screen time; "All of this material was unrehearsed and relatively unprepared. Photographic and acting quality: high".[30]

The first truly hot day was Monday, August 3. Anneke Wills, wife of Michael Gough, remembers Margaret Leighton emerging from make-up looking regal in a white full-length dress, swearing like a sailor that fruit flies had got under her wig.[31] But the heat wave turned out to be shortlived. The following week the scene of Leo's birthday party was shot. The Holt Fire Brigade was on hand to douse the windows with water to give the impression of

Getting ready for the picnic scene: Willem Ekels, Margaret Leighton, Julie Christie, Stephanie Kaye.

torrential rain. That Friday, Julie Christie went to dinner at Marsh Barn, bringing samphire she had gathered at Stiffkey with Terry Hodgkinson. Dominic was also there. "Don't become an actor," she told him, "do anything – doctor, anything – but an actor".[32]

The following week the dramatic scenes of Mrs Maudsley dragging Leo to the outhouse were filmed. The fire engines once again provided rain: "They were doing their best, but constantly getting into the picture," recorded Patricia.[33] The following day the weather seemed to clear and it was off to Heydon, an unspoilt village around a green some six miles from Melton, to do the scene of the church service. The first arrivals met with a hostile reception from the villagers: the previous week a crew from the television comedy series *Monty Python's Flying Circus* had appeared on the green, without permission, and filmed a sequence for episode 20. Once it became clear that they were the crew for *The Go-Between*, however, and that they did have permission, the attitude changed. They worked hard and Spike Priggen calculated that they managed to do three-and-a-half days of shooting in one day.

Filming the corn cutting at Hanworth. Left to right: Steve Smith, Mike Rutter (focus puller), Jerry Fisher, Richard Dalton, unidentified, Joseph Losey.

45

They were to return the next day to do the interior shots of the church. Terry Hodgkinson had arranged for four of the extras to act as bell ringers in the scene. They would be seen pulling ropes (dummies, which were attached to tractor tyres on beams high above them) with an open door as a backdrop. That evening, Terry was nervous – they should get real bell ringers for the scene. "I telephoned frantically around and managed to get two of Heydon's ringers to agree to show up at Melton the next morning at 6:30 to get into costume," he remembers. When Losey arrived at the church, he went up to one of the ringers and asked him: "You are a real bell ringer. How will you pull this rope?" Terry heaved a sigh of relief: "It was so like Joe," he says, "to assume that in this production the bell ringers would be real." After the film was released, Losey would receive a letter from a dedicated campanologist from Huntingdonshire who would point out that the peal of bells on the film's sound-track did not match the actions of the men's hands. It was one of the inherent problems with total realism.

That weekend the boys and their chaperone were lent a car to have a day in Norwich. The weather went back to rain. On Monday, August 17, Pinter arrived to be present at the shooting of the cricket match at Thornage, but rain forced them to do scenes in the outhouses at Melton and the party in the village hall instead. For the party, a large barn at Dairy Farm on the edge of the park at Melton was used. The interior was draped with flags and the piano on which Marian accompanied Ted in his Gilbert and Sullivan song was borrowed from Pauline Wiffen, daughter of Geoffrey Harrold, the owner of the hall. For complete authenticity, real beer in barrels was brought in from the Bell at Hunworth.

The rain turned to gales and continued to force them to postpone the cricket match. Interior scenes at Ted's farm were done at the two locations on the Hanworth estate which Carmen Dillon had chosen. About six miles from Melton, Meadow Farm provided the farmyard, while half a mile away a ramshackle house, since demolished, was transformed into Ted's farmhouse kitchen. Moura Budberg had arrived to stay with the Loseys and they all crowded behind the lights in the tiny room to watch. Then interiors were done in one of the houses on the green at Heydon: scaffolding had been erected outside to enable the camera to film through the window of a first-floor room. Transforming Julie Christie into the seventy-year-old Marian took several hours and involved making a mould of her face, which was then given wrinkles and make up and then applied to her face.

At last, on Wednesday, August 26, the weather cleared sufficiently to film the cricket match and the crew, all their equipment, extra hired costumes and props, and all the cast with the exception of Michael Redgrave, were mobilized for the most ambitious day of filming in the entire summer (see Chapter 1).

September 4 was a day filming in Norwich, inside the cathedral, as Leo looks up at the vastness of the Norman arches. A recording of the cathedral choir rehearsing would be dubbed in later. The weather continued cloudy and prevented any exterior shots being completed so the unit returned to Melton Constable and was dismissed. On Sunday the 6th they were back in Norwich, with Christie, Bates and Guard and a full complement of horses, carts, five coachmen and dozens of extras to film the horse auction scene. In Hartley's book, Leo is supposed to meet Marian after her errands by the statue of Sir Thomas Browne, near the market-place. An area that had been heavily bombed during the war, the site on inspection had been found to be hedged in by 1960s development and offering no convincing backdrops for the action. It was decided therefore to set the scene in Tombland, the ancient open space outside the gates of the Cathedral Close which had served as the

The horse fair on Tombland, Norwich: Marian (Julie Christie) and Ted (Alan Bates) spied in the distance.

market-place before the Normans had laid out a new one to the south of the Saxon settlement. It was here from the Middle Ages until well into the twentieth century that an annual horse fair had taken place. Zooming in and out with the camera lens, which had become a popular feature in films of the late 1960s, was felt by Losey to be best used sparingly ("they were not very smooth", remembers Steve Smith, "we didn't have the technical equipment in 1970").[34] In this scene it is used with shocking and powerful effect as one's eyes are taken past the auctioneer to catch a fleeting glimpse of Marian in the background, talking to a man who raises his hat as she walks away. The man is of course Ted Burgess.

The auctioneer for the scene was a real practitioner, Hubert Sheringham, a partner in the Norwich firm Irelands. Frank, the barman at the Feathers in Holt, a popular watering hole for the cast and crew, had been enlisted to play a soldier among the crowds. The crowded arrangement of unsaddled horses and onlookers was clearly much influenced by Sir Alfred Munnings's paintings of horse fairs in the early decades of the century. Perhaps the only scene in the film that is not taken from the book, it provides a colourful and dramatic interlude.

The sun, unfortunately, would not come out and the crew were forced to retreat inside again, this time into the Oak Room of the Maid's Head Hotel on Tombland to film the scenes of Marian and Leo having lunch. Bob Manning, head chef of Boswell's Restaurant on Tombland, had been hired to carve the beef in the scene but the staff of the Maid's Head objected strongly to the presence of someone from a rival establishment in the scene. "Bit of a cheek to use someone else when they are coming to our place," remarked Wildfred Duthaler, the hotel's own head chef. John Heyman, visiting for the day, tactfully replaced Manning with Peter Smith, another chef from the hotel's kitchen, who had the requisite beard and heavy girth.

Also visiting for the day were Bryan Forbes and Warren Beatty. When Beatty, who would be listed in the full credits of the film when it was released as "Industry Observer", was asked by a reporter why he was there, he replied: "just here to see Julie".

After shooting the scenes of Marian and Leo entering through the inn's courtyard, Losey decided to abandon the day's shooting as it looked unlikely that the sun would come out. There was no choice but to attempt the horse fair scene again later in the week. The horses and carts were loaded into lorries and the extras changed back into civilian clothes. The staff at Boswell's, still smarting at the slight they felt they had received, complained that the day's set-up had prevented customers from entering their restaurant.

But Losey and Priggen had other, more important, worries. Time was getting critically short, as shooting had to be completed by the end of the following week. According to the schedule, the next day it was to be the bathing scene, at Hickling Broad about ten miles north east of Norwich. In the book, the scene takes place on a swelteringly hot day, but the reality of Tuesday, September 7 was a biting wind and grey, overcast skies. An added problem was that the water in the broad was so shallow that swimming in it was virtually impossible. Nonetheless, Losey persevered. The wind noise in the microphone would later be carefully removed from the soundtrack by Peter Handford and replaced with the sound of insects and birds, giving the impression of a hot summer's day. There was nothing that could be done, however, with the grey reflection of the clouds on the water, or the waves whipped up by the stiff wind. Filming was delayed by the appearance of a motor cruiser, no doubt attracted by all the commotion, which promptly got itself grounded on a mud bank directly in camera shot. The combined efforts of the crew and Alan Bates finally freed it and shooting was resumed.

On return to Melton Constable, the parts of the two brothers, Simon Hume-Kendall and Richard Gibson, had been completed, as had those of Roger Lloyd Pack and Amaryllis Garnett, and they left amid tearful farewells. The party was starting to break up.

The following day, the menacing skies and rain proved to be less of a problem as the scenes to be shot were those of Leo's birthday party in which Mrs Maudsley, in driving rain, forces Leo to take her to the place where Marian and Ted are making love. Luckily, some of the flash forward scenes were to be shot on Thursday, and the continuing grey weather was just what was needed. Alan Bates's younger brother John, an art student, arrived to play the brief part of Ted Burgess's grandson.

On Friday, September 10 the whole crew with animals and extras were back in Norwich to film the auction scene. With that completed, it was Alan Bates's turn to say good-bye, but for the crew the day was not over as they had to move to Thorpe Station half a mile away to film Michael Redgrave, as the older Leo, leaving his train and being met by a chauffeur in one of the flash-forward scenes. In the final editing, these scenes at the station were not used: one merely sees Redgrave's hired car leaving the front of the station.

Shooting in the courtyard of the Maid's Head Hotel, Norwich. Left to right: Dudley Lovell, Joseph Losey, Julie Christie, Mike Rutter, Richard Dalton, unidentified.

Back at Melton Constable things really were winding down; some of the furniture had already been packed away and parts of the house were slowly returning to its deep slumber. Returning from the weekend, the crew had only Dominic Guard to shoot in a few linking scenes in the outhouses and on the lawns and Michael

A snapshot of Julie Christie saying good-bye to Camilla Farmer and Gerry Gavigan.

Redgrave inside Lady Trimingham's house at Heydon. On Wednesday, September 14 the last scenes were completed, a motley selection of short shots needed for continuity, along the drive, outside the house and back at the cricket pitch. At Thornage, Steve Smith, the clapper/loader, had to don cricket gear and fumble a catch. Amid tears, the party had truly come to an end. Steve presented Dominic with the clapper board. Losey gave him the Lincoln-green suit which Marian bought for him in Norwich.

As they watched the last rushes in the projection room at Melton, there was a distinct sadness in the air. Spike Priggen had to oversee the efficient and careful return of the props and costumes. He wrote a letter to the editor of the *Eastern Daily Press* "to express the sincere appreciation of both myself and Joseph Losey to the people of Norfolk who contributed so much to the filming ...", concluding that "the making of any successful film is a team affair; the people of Norfolk at all levels have been part of that team, and in every sense *The Go-Between* is as much their film as it is ours".[35] Terry Hodgkinson packed up his 2CV, now with the hatchback restored, and drove back to London feeling sad. "I really had been to that foreign country where they do things differently," he observed.[36]

Without exception, everyone, cast and crew alike, would remember the summer in glowing terms. Margaret Leighton had confided to a reporter that having such a happy time had worried her: "[T]he times I really enjoyed shooting on location, the film turned out to be a flop, but we needn't worry with this one".[37] Years later, Roger Lloyd Pack would reflect on that happy summer: "[Y]ou worry, if you lose some edge, some muscle".[38] But everyone felt that they were creating something that would be a landmark. "People gave an extra ten per cent," remembers Terry Hodgkinson.

Losey was meticulous in writing thank-you letters to everyone after shooting was over. He advised Dominic Guard, "If you finally decide to become an actor, I would suggest that you get a print of the Go-Between and run it at least once a year for the rest of your life to remind yourself how pure your art was when you were fourteen. This is not to imply you may not get better, but unfortunately so many people get worse, particularly when they start at such a high peak". To Julie Christie he wrote: "The picture looks good and you look superb. It was a happy picture and I enjoyed working with you, although between us we make a strange pair of non-communicators – however I think I got your messages and I hope you got mine". She wrote back, "It was a lovely, lovely film. I hope it left you as happy – and sad – as it left me. Thank you very, very much for persisting in the first place".[39] Christie was one of a small group of artists, mostly women, with whom Losey was never able to achieve total *rapport*.

Losey wrote to Carmen Dillon saying, "I cannot imagine anyone doing *The Go-Between* better than you have done". Dillon's response outlined her own frustrations of the summer: "my nose was rubbed so sorely in the non-schedule, the non-money and petty local crises that often the film proper, your film, disappeared behind an irritable migraine and drifted further and further away". Thus speaks the highly-strung perfectionist. She was only a year older than Losey and had designed her first film in 1939, so she felt able to be frank with him. On New Year's Eve she would write to him, "Please Joe don't go academic again. Nice for the students but sad for us".

Losey told Richard Dalton that he would now put him "in the unique category of absolutely top-drawer first assistants", and told Terry Hodgkinson that he was "a superb Second and a charming adjunct to the company", regretting the "destruction" of his "very personally engaging car". Losey thanked Roger Lloyd Pack for being part of "what, in this case was indeed, the family". Edward Fox declared in a letter to Losey that "it was enchanting work". Losey also received many letters from the crew, no doubt hopeful of future work, but all wrote with a genuine and deep-felt affection for the summer.[40] Pamela Davies, his trusted continuity girl, wrote to him of "the idyll of Norfolk".

1 Losey, interview in *Vogue*, October 15, 1970.
2 Steve Smith, interview with CH, April 12, 2011.
3 JWL/1/18/11.
4 Wilson, pp. 5–6.
5 Bailey, p. 14.
6 Stephanie Kaye, interview with CH, August 11, 2011.
7 Losey, interview with Anglia Television, August 28, 1970.
8 Taylor, p. 202.
9 Ciment, p. 312.
10 JWL/1/18/11.
11 Memorandum, Heyman to Hugh Sampson [in charge of publicity] and Losey, July 14, 1970, JWL/1/18/13.
12 Ewbank and Hildred, p. 175.
13 Fry, p. 284.
14 Ciment, p. 310.
15 Steve Smith, interview with CH, April 12, 2011.
16 Dominick Harrod, interview with CH, May 2, 2011.
17 Terry Hodgkinson, interview with CH, April 12, 2011.
18 Terry Hodgkinson, letter to CH, March 31, 2011.
19 PL, July 22, 1970.
20 Margaret Leighton, interview in *Women's Weekly*, October 21, 1971.
21 Roger Lloyd Pack, interview with CH, March 23, 2011.
22 Edward Fox, interview with CH, August 11, 2011; De Rham, p. 235.
23 Losey, interview in *Vogue*, October 15, 1970.
24 John Loring, quoted in Caute, p. 258.
25 Hayward, p. 110.
26 Julia Hull (*née* Howlett), interview with CH, March 12, 2011.
27 PL, July 19, 1970.
28 PL, July 31, 1970.
29 Fox, p. 123; Edward Fox, interview with CH, August 11, 2011.
30 JWL/1/18/13, box 3.
31 Wills, *Self Portrait*, p. 292.
32 Dominic Guard, interview with CH, August 3, 2011.
33 PL, August 12, 1970.
34 Steve Smith, interview with CH, April 12, 2011.
35 *Eastern Daily Press*, September, 1970.
36 Terry Hodgkinson, letter to CH, April 27, 2011.
37 Margaret Leighton, interview in *Women's Weekly*, October 21, 1971.
38 Roger Lloyd Pack, interview with CH, March 23, 2011.
39 JWL/1/18/14.
40 JWL/1/18/13.

4 RELEASE

JOSEPH AND PATRICIA STAYED ON in Norfolk for a few weeks. They had grown to love the county and were determined to find a house there. In the meantime, Losey signed an extension to the lease of Marsh Barn with the owner, Douglas Russell-Roberts. On September 29, Joseph and Patricia were married at King's Lynn Registry Office, with Harold Pinter and Baroness Moura Budberg as witnesses. For a week or so Losey recharged his batteries at the edge of the marsh. They saw Lord and Lady Zuckerman and Lady Sylvia Combe. Lord Leicester would drop in for a drink at sunset. They had dinner with Billa Harrod at Holt Rectory and discussed the parlous state of Melton Constable Hall. Losey offered to write to the National Trust, or Whitehall, to draw attention to its condition. In October he received a response from the Ministry of Housing and Local Government, which he forwarded to Harrod: "The Ministry has been concerned for a number of years about this building".[1]

For Losey and the editing and sound crew, there was still much to be done to make a film out of all the footage they had shot that summer. The editor, Reginald Beck, and his assistants worked at Elstree piecing the action together, and Peter Handford and his team dubbed in sounds. Handford was a quiet, soft-spoken man who lived in Suffolk, where he made recordings of wild life as well as of steam trains. His approach to historical sound was as meticulous as Losey's was to authenticity in props and settings. In a memorandum he had written to Losey earlier in the summer, he said that:

> Because of the lower overall level of "noise" in the Edwardian period, in relation to the
> present day, the sounds in the countryside were much more definitive that they are now.
> Many older country people, and county-townspeople, still have very definitive memories of

sounds, mostly now gone or at best submerged, which formed a background to their lives and can, without prompting, give quite graphic details of sounds which they remember ... It seems doubtful whether in 30–50 years' time, the older people will have anything like the same memories of sounds which they now know; the dominant sounds of present-day life are almost without exception harsh, unrhythmical, and overloud by comparison.[2]

Carmen Dillon was continuing to fret about the deadly nightshade, which she felt looked dead and unconvincing even in the scenes shot day-for-night. She experimented at Elstree with more of the plant brought in from the Royal Botanic Gardens at Kew, and some shots were filmed which were cut into the outhouse scenes.

The Loseys' Norfolk vacation was cut short in October with the arrival in London of James Aubrey, head of MGM, who earlier in the year had purchased a half share in the film – but had yet to pay for it. Aubrey was demanding to see the rough cut. Patricia recorded in her diary: "Joe said no to John Heyman, who said no to Bryan Forbes, who said no to Bernie Delfont, who said no to Mr Aubrey. Mr Aubrey said, right then, no money for The Go-Between. Mr D *ordered* Mr F to show it. Mr F rang Mr H who rang Joe, who said bitterly: okay. They saw some bits last night and only Mr Aubrey is reported to like it".[3] The truth was that Aubrey thought it was the "best still picture he'd ever seen" and suggested drastic cuts before boarding his plane. Heyman and Priggen merely suggested that the exorcism scene was unclear.

Undeterred, Losey and his team continued editing and a couple of weeks later, a new cut was screened. Pinter and L.P. Hartley were in the audience. Patricia noted in her diary that "a few weeks ago there seemed something lacking. This time no. My reservations about certain details remain, but now I think the film transcends them – has found its proper rhythm. Sat next to Harold and behind Leslie Hartley. I was conscious of Harold observing Leslie's reactions as I observed them myself. From the very first line: 'The past is a foreign country. They do things differently there' it was clear that Leslie was moved and *that* was exciting and moving".[4]

The question of music in the film had to be addressed. Richard Rodney Bennett had composed the music for several of Losey's films, each score vastly different in approach and feeling – including *Secret Ceremony*, a claustrophobic psychological thriller which had starred Mia Farrow, and *Figures in a Landscape*, the film which Losey had completed just prior to starting *The Go-Between*. Bennett had also written the score for *Far from the Madding Crowd* in 1967, so he was seen by Delfont as a bankable artist. But Losey's idea of what music in a film should be was quite different from Bennett's: "Joseph Losey is one of the good guys, except that he has a mysterious belief of what music could do and say to an audience. Music can say all sorts of things that you can't put into words. Losey used to say to me 'I want the music to be telling the audience that Elizabeth Taylor is thinking this and Mia Farrow that ...' That's not what music does! So he was difficult. But music was so important to him, it wasn't just dressing".[5]

In October Bennett flew in from Baltimore, where he was doing a visiting professorship, to see the rough cut of *The Go-Between*. Bennett returned to Baltimore and in two weeks had completed a score which he recorded in a London studio. Losey was disappointed: it was not what he imagined the music could be, but was at a loss to tell Bennett just what that was. He cabled Bennett: "Music is obviously first-class but neither music or musical effects are really right. Stop. Believe everything must be redone from scratch. Stop. What do you suggest? Could you do something electronic? Or jazz?" Bennett's reply was accommodating and polite.

But in December Bennett wrote to Losey again from Baltimore: "I never really got a mental picture of what the music ought to do. I would dearly love to try again, but must admit that I am no clearer in my mind. I even have a sneaking feeling that it ought not to have *any* music ... I think the sanest thing is for me to get out and let you either get someone else in, or do the picture without music and if possible 'heighten' the sound effects where necessary". Losey wrote back, thanking him for his "extraordinarily generous letter" and promised to respond to him soon. In the meantime Losey had also approached Harrison Birtwhistle as well as the Suffolk composer Tristram Carey. Losey wanted music that wouldn't "get in the way" and he still thought a jazz score, possibly electronic, could work. Delfont and the others, though, were less than enthusiastic.

To link in with the song that Ted sings after the cricket match, a Gilbert and Sullivan score was suggested. Handford recalled: "Joe was aghast, rising out of his chair, declaring that the last thing he'd ever do would be to use G. and S., like some high-school production".[6] In desperation, Losey countered with the suggestion of no music at all. "Totally uncommercial" was the verdict of the money men. So finally it was the French composer Michel Legrand, who had done the music to Losey's *Eve*, who was hired by Losey to write a new score.

After Christmas, Losey cabled Bennett again: "Cannot get any agreement to delivering the picture without any music therefore Michel Legrand is undertaking a new score. Very sorry and sure we will work together again soon. Best wishes Joe Losey." André Previn, who had written fifty-seven film scores and had experienced his own rejections, rang Bennett up to say: "Welcome to the club!"[7]

Legrand arrived in London on January 6 to stay with the Loseys and was shown a rough cut of the film. He delivered a complete score – a short, strident theme, with eleven variations, with overtones of Satie – in record time. Losey's initial reaction was negative; Legrand refused to re-do it and left London, leaving Losey, Beck, Handford and Craven to deal with it. They made it work: the music in the finished film is loud and uncompromising, and continues to provoke extreme reactions to this day – audiences either love it or hate it.

In the meantime Peter Handford, for whom the glass was always half empty, was unhappy about the way some of the editing was being done; in November he had written to Losey that "a lot of the atmosphere and style has gone from the film in its present form, certainly the style is different from early versions".[8] The present-day scenes continued to raise some doubts. Reginald Beck had voiced his concerns with Losey when he read the screenplay in 1969, and he felt that the cricket and picnic scenes were too long. Others at EMI agreed – what would the US audiences make of the cricket scene? Losey and Pinter were adamant that the scene should remain in, but agreed to trim the picnic, although Losey observed that "somehow I think its leisurely pace is necessary and also it *does* convey the emptiness of those lives".[9]

Patricia left for Brazil to visit her two children. "The Joe I found on my return was more like the Joe I had first known at the time of *Eve*. Jagged, he seemed to have fallen to pieces – nervy, jumpy, shaken with tremors and asthma". Losey's friend and agent Robin Fox had died, and he was in that loathsome barren time between

Bell ringers in Heydon church, with Mrs Maudsley entering. The ringers were real, but the ropes were attached to tractor tyres in the roof.

projects. Norfolk beckoned. "That spring and summer we spent a lot of time at Brancaster, where we were happy. Brancaster was the only place Joe felt happy alone, even without a car when I had to go off for a couple of days to London. Brancaster was very special for both of us," she noted.[10]

Their sojourn at Brancaster was interrupted with disquieting news about *The Go-Between*. The feared James Aubrey had re-entered the fray. Nicknamed the "Smiling Cobra", Aubrey had fired 3,500 employees at MGM in his efforts to streamline the operation. His approach to films was equally clinical. He was not impressed by *The Go-Between* and saw it as difficult to sell to American audiences. On the other hand, Bryan Forbes at EMI, who had pronounced Pinter's script the finest he had ever read, saw the film as just the kind of quality production that EMI should be making. But Forbes's boss Bernard Delfont was only lukewarm. Forbes recalled:

> "It's mostly about the boy," he told me incredulously as if through some strange process
> hitherto unknown to man Losey had managed to distort Hartley's original plot.
> "Yes," I said, "the go-between."
> "Well," said Bernie, "he runs forever, for miles and miles."[11]

Years later, Delfont, by then Lord Delfont, would remember the film as "sheer joy", "closer to the European than to the American style of film-making" and one which was warmly received by "the sort of audiences who had almost given up their local cinema as a lost cause".[12]

Forbes and Losey had enjoyed an uneasy professional relationship: Forbes regarded Losey as difficult but respected his professionalism on the set. Given Losey's reputation in France, and the artistic brilliance of the film, Forbes felt it would be an ideal entry into the Cannes Film Festival. Lobbying began to make *The Go-Between* Britain's official entry. But word came from Hollywood that Aubrey was preparing to premiere the film in Los Angeles, in a small art cinema in the suburb of Westwood, close to UCLA. Opening outside its country of origin would disqualify the film for Cannes. Forbes remonstrated but was rebuffed by Aubrey, who poured scorn on the film's prospects at Cannes. Furthermore, Pinter and Losey had no commercial appeal, he said. Forbes stood his ground and refused to release the final cut to MGM. The film was shown to the cast and crew at the Warwick cinema on April 5, and opened at the Hanover Grand in London on May 7. Among those invited were

Luchino Visconti and Joseph Losey in an awkward encounter prior to the Palme d'Or awards ceremony in Cannes. The Go-Between won, beating Visconti's Death in Venice by a single vote.

all the cast and many from Norfolk, including Lord Leicester, Sylvia Combe, Lady Hastings, the Harrods, the Harrolds, Jack Carter and even the Mad Hatter from Weybourne. Billa Harrod wrote enthusiastically to Losey afterwards: "It was the most thrilling evening and surpassed even the expectations we have been living on since the summer ... it is lovely to see the Norfolk countryside and Norfolk buildings so sympathetically shown".[13] Her only criticism of the film, which she confided to her son, was that the two boys should have removed their hats at the front door when they arrived at the beginning of the film, not in their bedroom upstairs.[14]

By the time of the premiere, however, Forbes had left EMI, his brief reign as the "White Knight of the British film industry" over. The headline in the *Evening News* announced "Family Film Man Forbes is Sacked".[15] Forbes had hoped to make Britain a centre of quality film-making but the end of the era when British films were seen as chic in America had coincided with drastic falls in cinema-going in Britain. Art and commerce parted ways once again, but at least *The Go-Between* had been saved from premature burial on the American art-house circuit. Clearly anxious to be rid of it, Aubrey sold the US distribution rights to Columbia for a meagre £250,000.

The competition for the Palme d'Or at Cannes that year was tough. *The Go-Between* was announced as the British entry, but only after Losey had diligently lobbied the critic and jury member, Dilys Powell. The Italian entry was Luchino Visconti's *Death in Venice* starring Dirk Bogarde, who had appeared in a number of Losey's films in the early 1960s. It was widely agreed that Bogarde had developed from a shallow matinee idol into a mature actor of great sensitivity under Losey's direction. But after *Accident* in 1966, Losey had, much to

Bogarde's disgust, entered his Burton/Taylor period and the two friends had drifted apart. Arriving at the Colombe d'Or for the festival, the Loseys were presented with flowers and a card from Bogarde welcoming them and adding "I hope you don't win!" Bogarde felt *The Go-Between* was good but not great art like *Death in Venice*. He waspishly criticized the costumes, and described the boys' accents as "very Earls Court".[16]

It was clearly going to be a two-horse race, between two "art" directors with very similar styles but wildly differing backgrounds. Not long after, Losey and Pinter would find their project to film Proust coming head to head with Visconti's own plans. At Cannes, the allegations flew that Visconti was trying to bribe members of the jury and that he promised one of them a part in his next film.[17] Finally, at the eleventh hour, Erich Segal was the casting vote and *The Go-Between* was declared the winner. According to Bogarde, as soon as word had got out about the verdict, Visconti packed his luggage and left for Rome, but was lured back from the airport by the promise of a hurriedly arranged "Special Award".[18] The two directors came face to face before the ceremony and awkwardly shook hands. John Heyman spent the evening in the casino rather than at the ceremony, as Delfont had decided to accept the award himself "for a film he had almost managed to derail".[19] The telegrams and letters poured in – from Bryan Forbes, from the Harrods, from Phyllis the housekeeper at Melton Constable.

Julie Christie had not been present at Cannes, but she and Warren Beatty did appear at the charity screening held at the Museum of Modern Art in New York on July 29. She had written to Losey in May after she saw the film in London: "[I]t's a lovely, lovely picture. If I didn't hate phoning so much I would have phoned you before

I left. I'm pleased with myself, too, which is incredibly rare. I don't think I had a single cringe. I usually don't see my movies, or hide in the loo half the time during particularly embarrassing bits of myself. So many thanks, Mister, for getting me to do it".[20] Shortly after Cannes the film opened in France to widespread praise. John Heyman reported that it looked likely to be among the five biggest earners for that year. When Losey attended the Belgian premiere: the magazine *Pourquoi Pas* headed their review "Merci, M. McCarthy!" referring to Losey's blacklisting and exile nearly twenty years before.

The film's release in New York sparked almost unanimous acclaim. Judith Crist declared it "a film of such taste, so deeply compassionate and wryly sophisticated, so subtle and literate and aware of the universalities of its very special time and place – no wonder some movie mogul felt its box-office possibilities were nil!".[21] Vincent Canby of the *New York Times* declared that it was "one of the few movies, in fact, that I can recommend without any real qualification".[22] Gene Shalit observed that Dominic Guard was "that rare treasure, a good child actor".[23] The only dissenting voice seemed to be David Goldman of WCBS Newsradio, who described the film as "a very romantic turn-of-the-century drama of class conflicts in England. Perhaps to an English audience, or to an American with English sensibility, there is more drama and suspense in this kind of material".[24]

This lone voice of dissent, however, uncannily echoed the ennui about parts of the film that had developed in London while Losey and the cast promoted the film in New York. John Heyman wanted more cuts. When he saw the list of proposed cuts, Pinter said "John's gone mad".[25] The main point of concern was the present-day scenes, with their mixing up of the chronology. In response Pinter wrote to Heyman: "*The Go-Between* is a very densely organised piece of film-making, considered and executed with the greatest care and the finest sensitivity, both as regards formal rhythm and balanced content. If certain distributors feel that the film needs cutting they will do whatever they do, it seems to me, in accordance with their own standard of values and at their own risk. For any of us to anticipate such action by taking the action ourselves I consider a wretched posture, and one which would clearly demonstrate a basic lack of confidence in the film as conceived and executed, a posture doubly ironic in view of the great success the film has already achieved".[26]

Heyman remained sceptical, but the film that was put on general release in Britain in September was essentially the same cut as that shown in New York. The English critics were also unstinting in their praise: "one of those films that reinforce one's faith in the cinema", Michael Billington had declared in July.[27] Others joined in the chorus. John Russell Taylor, who had visited the shoot for *Sight and Sound*, was wholehearted in his praise: "Visually the film is a constant joy, summoning up perfectly the image of baking summer and the tranquil surface of upper-class Edwardian England, beneath which ungovernable passions lurk".[28] George Melly, though, writing in the *Observer*, criticized the elder brother's gaucheness. But surely that was what was intended? Other critics put the film's depiction of class under a microscope: Araminta Wordsworth observed: "Though strictly speaking most of the characters in L.P. Hartley's novel are not aristocratic, they are nouveaux-riches and the big house in Norfolk is perhaps a mite too ostentatious in its luxury and splendours as is their awareness of the gulf between them and 'the village'. The eldest son of the house shows this clearly in his gauche assumption of the role of *noblesse oblige*; his lack of true aristocratic fibre is shown up by the behaviour of a real aristocrat, Viscount Trimingham, Marian's fiancé".[29]

The offending poster to promote the film in the United Kingdom. John Heyman dubbed it a "cheap soap powder campaign".

Gauche is perhaps the best word to describe the promotional campaign that launched *The Go-Between* in Britain. Posters and advertisements showed the three main characters drawn in the style of a pulp paperback and announced "In those days, you fell in love with your own class. Or found a Go-Between". Losey, Pinter and Heyman were appalled. On September 23, Heyman wrote to Delfont, asking to be disassociated from this "cheap soap powder campaign". Delfont promised to give Losey's name and the Palme d'Or more prominence. In the end, the United Kingdom receipts were to be just under £300,000 compared to Columbia's combined gross takings in America and France of £1,375,300.[30] The Society of Film and Television Arts awarded *The Go-Between* four BAFTAs: Pinter for Best Screenplay; Margaret Leighton for Best Supporting Actress; Edward Fox for Best Supporting Actor, and Dominic Guard as Most Promising Newcomer. Sadly, the film lost out to John Schlesinger's *Sunday Bloody Sunday* for Best Film. Though nominated for an Academy Award, *The Go-Between* failed to win. Losey felt it was because of a lack of any effective campaign in Hollywood.

After the March preview in London, Billa Harrrod had written to Losey suggesting the idea of a charity premiere in Norwich, citing ingenuously a charity screening of *Death in Venice* which had benefited Venice in Peril. With his support she set about organizing the event for October, to benefit Norwich churches and the Campaign for the Preservation of Rural England. By May she had "laid a few trails towards the Royal Family" to secure a guest of honour.[31] In early October Losey was writing to Bryan Forbes: "I hope you go to the Royal Performance at Norwich and make your presence uncomfortably felt. Why don't you arrive with The Queen Mother?"[32]

Crowds gather outside the ABC Cinema in Norwich for the "Royal Screening" of The Go-Between, *October 29, 1971.*

The "Royal Screening" took place at the ABC Cinema in Prince of Wales Road, Norwich, on October 29, 1971, in the presence of H.M. The Queen Mother, who stayed with Sir Edmund and Lady Bacon at Raveningham Hall. The event was a glittering affair with some thirteen hundred guests including the Lord Mayor of Norwich, the Bishop of Norwich, many local notables and members of the cast. The Mad Hatter arrived in opera cloak and silk top hat. Young people dressed in costumes from the film acted as ushers. Dominick Harrod remembers sitting in the row behind The Queen Mother: "I saw the entire film through her diamond tiara," he said.[33] L.P. Hartley finally managed to come to Norfolk, and stayed with Billa Harrod. Before the performance he, Harold Pinter, Dominic Guard, Edward Fox and Patricia Losey were presented to The Queen Mother by Bernard Delfont. Losey himself was away on location shooting his next feature, *The Assassination of Trotsky*, in Mexico City. He sent a telegram to Patricia: "Love to all the friends in the home town and you".[34] Afterwards, there was a civic supper held in the newly built rotunda in Norwich Castle. Patricia and the others stayed at the Maid's Head, scene of Marian's lunch with Leo.

Shortly afterwards, to her surprise, Billa Harrod received a bill from Delfont for £535.28 for hire of the cinema. She sent it back to him, explaining: "Norfolk landscape (which we exist to protect) playing such a huge part in the film – *and* the vast publicity we gave it".[35] Losey wrote to her saying that he could not help her, "as my numerous letters to Delfont produce only more and more insipid evasions … I believe with your name and position, and Delfont's desire for a knighthood, you can shame him into submission".[36] A few days after the screening Losey had cabled Delfont: "Delighted your success at Norwich. Stop. Regret to inform you that Italian release disgraceful …" The battle continued.

In the draft of his 1976 essay for Angus Wilson's anthology of East Anglian writing, Losey gave vent to his anger at Delfont's backing out of the project in 1968 and again in 1969: "[T]he distributor, who later claimed all credit for the film's success at Cannes (Grand Prix) and who used our work quite shamelessly to promote his

Harold Pinter and L.P. Hartley are presented to H.M. The Queen Mother by Bernard Delfont.

own elevation to the peerage, had reneged on a signed contract; the leading actors, the writer, the active producer and I were all forced to work for little and sometimes nothing and to squeeze ourselves into a much reduced schedule to achieve our work".[37] But they had wrought a masterpiece.

1 RHP, f. 92.
2 JWL/1/18/13 box 3.
3 PL, October 10, 1970.
4 PL, October 24, 1970.
5 Meredith, p. 188.
6 De Rham, p. 254.
7 Meredith, p. 216.
8 JWL/1/18/13 box 3.
9 Losey to Pinter, October 8, 1970, JWL/1/18/14.
10 Patricia Losey, unpublished memoir.
11 Forbes, p. 100.
12 Delfont, p. 120.
13 Lady Harrod to Losey, May 14, 1971, JWL/1/18/12.
14 Dominick Harrod, interview with CH, May 2, 2011.
15 March 25, 1971.
16 Caute, p. 230.
17 Ibid., p. 273.
18 Ibid., p. 274.
19 Ibid., p. 274.
20 Christie to Losey, May 18, 1971, JWL/1/18/14.
21 *NY Magazine*, July 26, 1971.

22 *New York Times*, July 30, 1971.
23 WNBC-TV News, July 29, 1971.
24 WCBS Newsradio 88, July 29, 1971.
25 Patricia Losey to Losey, memorandum, n.d., [July 1971], JWL/1/18/14.
26 Pinter to Heyman, July 21, 1971, JWL/1/18/14.
27 *Illustrated London News*, July, 1971.
28 "The shadows of a country house summer", *Times*, September 24, 1971.
29 *Times Educational Supplement*, September 1, 1971.
30 Caute, p. 277.
31 Lady Harrod to Losey, May 24, 1971, JWL/1/18/6.
32 Losey to Forbes, October 11, 1971, JWL/1/18/13.
33 Dominick Harrod, interview with CH, May 2, 2011.
34 JWL/1/18/6.
35 Lady Harrod to Patricia Losey, November 14, 1971, JWL/1/18/13.
36 Losey to Lady Harrod, November 30, 1971, JWL/1/18/16.
37 Losey draft, dated September 13, 1976, JWL/1/18/8.

5 LEGACY

IN DECEMBER 1971, *THE GO-BETWEEN* delighted winter audiences with its evocation of a long, hot summer. Showing at the cinema in Fakenham, a few miles from Melton Constable, the film was held up one evening because, the management announced, Michael Gough (now living in nearby Field Dalling) was on his way. During the 1972 flat-racing season a horse named *The Go-Between*, ridden by Lester Piggott, enjoyed some success.

The "time play" in the film does not appear to have confused audiences as much as Heyman and Delfont had feared, although the elderly James Lees-Milne, watching the film in October, 1971, noted in his diary; "I am constantly amazed at the historical ignorance of people who should know better. For instance, in the beautiful Go-Between film, motor cars dating from the 1930s were allowed to appear in Norwich Close in what was meant to be Edwardian times".[1] The verdict on Burgess's Norfolk accent was generally positive (he had been coached by Dick Joice, the presenter of Anglia Television's programme *Bygones*), but one viewer wrote to Losey pointing out that Burgess used the expression "so long" – an Americanism of the 1940s.

Michael Gough with George Grieff, the gardener, at Melton Constable Hall, the photograph inscribed: "My friend George, we are acting our parts well. Who would know that we were really mates. Best wishes and thank you, Michael Gough".

Nonetheless, *The Go-Between* set new standards of historical accuracy, which would influence film and television in the years to come. Realism on its own can be stultifying, as some of the period television work of the 1970s and 80s demonstrates, but the depth of the plot and the characters of *The Go-Between* have ensured the continuing popularity of the film. Adopted as a National Curriculum text in schools, the book continues to sell in large numbers, and this in turn has influenced sales of the DVD and Blu-ray of the film. In the mid-1990s the book was adapted for the stage and in September 2011 a musical version opened at the West Yorkshire Playhouse in Leeds. Hartley's reputation grows as Pinter's diminishes somewhat. As one

"Judging a film director by watching him work on the set is like writing about an architect by observing a building site" *John Boorman, 1983*

astute writer observed at the time of Hartley's death in 1972: "[C]ritics who praised Harold Pinter's script for *The Go-Between* did not always realize the extent to which the best – and often the most Pinteresque – things in it were, in fact, Hartley's."[2] Hartley's economy of dialogue, for instance, meshed well with Pinter's own approach to the use of words.

Ambiguities in the film continue to perplex audiences. For example, it is never made clear that Trimingham is the owner of Brandham Hall and its estate. Other ambiguities are intentional. What are Trimingham's true motives? Does he really love Marian, or is he just hoping to save the estate with Mr Maudsley's cash? We suspect but cannot be certain that he knows of Marian's affair with Ted. At the end of the film, does the older Leo indeed carry out Marian's last errand? In Hartley's book, Leo goes to lunch but he plans to deliver quite a different message from the one Marian has given him. In the film, it is not even clear that Leo indeed enters Brandham Hall for a last time – as the house is reflected in the rain-splattered car window, is he about to drive away, free at last?

In the final scenes of the film, the house stands stark and lonely; the trees have been cut down in a metaphor of a lost social order. In the early 1970s no one knew that the English country house would enjoy such a renaissance in the final years of the century (perversely, though, Melton itself remains empty to this day).

Much as he did with an Art Nouveau house in *Secret Ceremony*, Losey gave Melton Constable Hall a role in *The Go-Between* that is every bit as powerful as that of the leading characters. Indeed, while Hartley's novel had described features of Brandham Hall in great detail – the staircase, the terrace, the gardens – and had sketched in aspects of the house's architecture, the house was not the key element it was to become under Losey's direction. "[T]he great house of *The Go-Between* did not conceal its destructiveness to the boy, or its cruelty or its boredom or inequalities of benevolent feudalism. Or the sterility of that way of life and the frustrations of its women. Or the suicide and the perverted or ruined lives," Losey wrote later.[3]

But the greatest role in the film was that played by the landscape itself. Hartley's novel just happens to be set in Norfolk. The reader is not treated to any elegiac descriptions celebrating the beauty of the setting, and the only time young Leo is aware that he is in Norfolk is when he crosses a field and notices that the straw has been stacked differently from the way it is done in Wiltshire. Pinter's screenplay makes only passing reference to location. But under Losey's direction, the beauty of north Norfolk comes to dominate the film. Losey's intention was that "the picture should look hot and like a slightly faded Renoir or Constable – the colours mostly gold and brown". From the first scene, as the camera passes through the raindrops trickling down the window (the dull present) into the ripe, golden cornfield, the audience is transported into a landscape of such beauty that it seems at once timeless and *timeful*.

Norfolk has gone on to play varied roles in film and television, either as itself, as in *The Ploughman's Lunch* (1983) or *Shadows in the Sun* (2010), or masquerading as another place, such as the Carolinas in *Shakespeare in Love* (1988), a North Korean paddy field in *Die Another Day* (2002), or Denmark in *Out of*

Africa (1985). Shortly after *The Go-Between* Melton Constable Hall itself played host to another film: *Our Miss Fred* starring the female impersonator, Danny La Rue. The shades of Mrs Maudsley must have been horrified. Among other Norfolk houses, Holkham Hall is in frequent demand as a location, and films and television work have been done at Heydon Hall (*The Grotesque*, 1995, which also starred Alan Bates) and Sennowe Park (*Dean Spanley*, 2008). Stephen Fry's television series *Kingdom*, set in and around Swaffham, made use of East Barsham Manor, Hindringham Hall and other houses. Julie Christie returned to Norfolk in 2008 to appear in *Glorious 39*, a film by Stephen Poliakoff, filmed at Walsingham Abbey and the surrounding countryside. This time she found it "as wild and windy as ever. I suppose the biggest change I noticed was the gentrification of the villages, both modest and grand".[4]

In many respects *The Go-Between* represents a turning point in British cinema, marking the end of the studio system. Smaller production units, foreign locations using local crews; developments such as these were becoming more common. The film's innovations – in filming entirely on location, and with complete authenticity – created challenges for the older members of the production crew, many of whom had been trained in the studio tradition. Carmen Dillon found it especially hard to shoot on location.[5]

Joe and Patricia Losey moved to Paris in 1975. In France, Losey was a god. With sadness, they gave up Marsh Barn and said good-bye to the north Norfolk landscape they had grown to love. Some of Losey's subsequent films, such as the masterly *Mr Klein*, a tense drama of mistaken identity in Nazi-occupied Paris, and his lavish, and idiosyncratic, adaptation of the opera *Don Giovanni,* received critical acclaim but none of his later films attained the perfection, or commercial success, of *The Go-Between*. Losey continued to be regarded as "difficult" by studio bosses, and all of his proposed American projects ultimately fell through. Although Pinter wrote a screenplay of Proust's *A la recherche du temps perdu*, he and Losey never succeeded in making the film. Losey died in 1984.

Today, Losey remains a larger-than-life figure, in part because his failures were as spectacular as his successes. Losey's stature as a director continues to rise as the fights with studio bosses, which have often distorted objective assessment of his films, fade into history. The British Film Institute's centenary retrospective on Losey's work in 2007 was the beginning of a new recognition of Losey as one of the great artists of the twentieth century.

The artist as human being, though, will always fascinate us. Losey in Norfolk showed one facet – a happy, productive one – of a very mixed and turbulent personality. "He seemed to have this vision", as one extra on *The Go-Between* cannily observed. He needed work to flourish. Only happy when he was practising his craft, Losey found in Norfolk an ideal environment for creativity.

Losey's lifestyle in the 1960s and 70s of glamorous locations and 5-star hotels seems to sit uneasily with his professed left-wing philosophy and with his work, which studies rigid class structures. Writing in 1976 of his love for Norfolk, he said: "No amount of lyricism or personal cherished memories, such as weekend shopping in Burnham Market, or a drink by the fire at the Jolly Sailor, or special pleasures or comforts, can conceal the fact that life for most people was and is hard. That there is much poverty, in spite of diligence".[6] But the tailor must be well-dressed, and money attracts money. The European film-making world during that period was very much part of the world he satirized in *Modesty Blaise* and *Boom*. Losey was fascinated by wealth and position; he loved to hear the reminiscences of past imperial grandeur of his friend Baroness Budberg, and his letters and writings are full of references to "my friend Lord Dynevor"[7] or "Tommy Coke, Earl of Leicester ... dear man, great crush on Julie Christie".[8] The artist as observer. It took Losey and Pinter, both outsiders, to dissect the English class system so brilliantly. The directness of approach also shows Losey's Mid-western origins. It comes through in his correspondence and one can see how it must sometimes have offended European sensibilities. Yet cast and crew of *The Go-Between* speak warmly of Losey as a colleague, and of his sensitivity as a director. Norfolk seemed to bring out the best in him.

What of the others? Some, like Michael Gough and Roger Lloyd Pack, acquired houses in north Norfolk in the wake of *The Go-Between*. Anneke Gough recalls: "We were very aware that it was the end of the 60s and we wanted to get out of London and live in the country; I found an idyllic eighteenth century farmhouse at Field Dalling".[9] Edward Fox and his new love, Joanna David, as well as Margaret Leighton and her husband, Michael Wilding, also considered buying houses in the area. In 1971, the Goughs, Lloyd Pack and Roddy Maude-Roxby, another actor and Norfolk immigrant, started an arts centre in Wells-next-the-Sea that would flourish for some years.

Norfolk too was coming to the end of one phase and already the beginnings of a new era were appearing. The post-war move to mechanization in farming, Norfolk's main industry, had put paid to thousands of rural jobs, and there were few new jobs being created in the manufacturing industries in Norwich. Rural poverty was a reality. In the meantime, the popularity of second homes, especially along the coast, accelerated during the 1970s. As early as 1971 the London *Evening Standard* reported that north Norfolk had become known as "the 'Gold Coast' among estate agents because of its booming sales market".[10] The new dawn of service and creative businesses operating in the rural quiet of the region would not come until the advent of the internet. But in many respects, north Norfolk today is unchanged from 1970, and 1900.

1 James Lees-Milne, *Diaries*, October 9, 1971, p. 18.
2 Francis King, Obituary of L.P. Hartley, *Sunday Telegraph*, December 17, 1972.
3 Wilson, pp. 7–8.
4 Julie Christie, e-mail to CH, September 2, 2011.
5 Taylor, p. 202.
6 Wilson, p. 7.
7 Losey to Norman Priggen, February 4, 1969, JWL/1/18/12.
8 Wilson, p. 7.
9 Anneke Wills, interview with CH, August 5, 2011.
10 "The Go-Between inspires new arts centre", *Evening Standard*, October 30, 1971.

Synopsis of the Film

Marcus tells Leo to throw his clothes on the floor for the servants to pick up; between them is the dog Dry Toast (stage name unknown).

Marcus and Leo on the staircase at Brandham Hall.

LEO COLSTON, who is spending the summer with his school chum Marcus, finds Brandham Hall, Norfolk, more than just a rather grand house: it is for him a place of enchantment.

For Marcus has an older sister, Marian, and 12-year-old Leo comes under her spell at their very first meeting.

The Hall, with its impressive staircase and its portraits, is for him a whole new world. There are plenty of servants, and life seems to revolve around a series of formal dinners, elaborate picnics and croquet on the lawn. He is, understandably, a little overawed by it all, but the house is large and there are several derelict summerhouses, overgrown with dense vegetation, for him to explore ...

In one of them grows a plant he recognises: a large glossy shrub with bell-shaped flowers. It is *atropa belladonna*, deadly nightshade.

At his very first dinner, Leo finds himself sitting next to Mrs Maudsley. "I believe we must be wary of

you, Leo" she tells him, "I understand you are a magician."

"His curses are fearful" Marcus tells them all. "He cast a fiendish spell on two boys at school. They fell off the roof and were severely mutilated."

Mr Maudsley then asks if it wasn't difficult to arrange.

"Well, it wasn't a killing curse, you see" Leo replies. "There are curses and curses."

"You're not going to bewitch us here, are you?" asks Marian, who already has poor Leo bewitched.

Leo soon realises that he hasn't the right clothes for such a hot summer, and it is Marian who takes him into Norwich to buy him a cool suit. She leaves him to amuse himself for a while and goes off. Leo later sees her in the distance talking to a man.

When they arrive home, Mrs Maudsley asks Marian if she has seen anyone in Norwich. "We were hard at it all the time, weren't we, Leo?" Marian replies. And Leo agrees. Later, at a bathing party organised by the youngsters, a powerful young stranger is seen swimming in the river. He is Ted Burgess, a tenant farmer.

When Marcus goes down with the measles, Leo is left rather to his own devices. Though he does become friendly with Viscount Trimingham, a newly-arrived guest at the Hall.

On one of his lonely afternoon walks, Leo wanders over by the river and finds a haystack to play on. He slides down, hitting his knee on a chopping block at the bottom. It is Ted's haystack, and it is he who dresses the wound.

When Ted learns that Leo is staying at the Hall, he asks him to take a letter to Marian. "We do some business together" he explains. He then swears him to secrecy. Leo likes Ted, and he loves Marian. He eventually agrees, and so becomes the *go-between*. Marian is naturally delighted, and this new intimacy pleases Leo, who spends his days carrying

Ted Burgess gives Leo another letter.

messages and checking the thermometer, which seems stuck in the nineties.

One day Marian, in her haste to get a message to Ted, hands Leo an unsealed letter. He is, without actually taking it out of its envelope, able to read some of it. When he realises it is a love letter, he is bitterly upset and angry – but also very curious.

He delivers the letter, but tells Ted he can no longer act as postman: Marcus has now recovered from the measles, he explains, and he won't be alone. Ted takes quite a tough line with Leo, telling him that Marian will stop liking him if he quits acting as "go-between".

Leo counters by asking Ted what lovers do together. Ted promises to tell him all about "spooning" if he will continue to carry messages. Leo agrees.

The annual cricket match, the Hall v. the Village, is a big day for Leo. Not only is Marian among the spectators, but she sees him make a brilliant catch that ends the hard-hitting Ted's innings. That night at the concert, Leo, hero of the cricket match, is acclaimed for his singing. But his wildly happy mood ends abruptly later that evening when he is told by Marcus that Marian's engagement to Hugh Trimingham is about to be announced.

It is, for Leo, the last straw. But when he tells Marian that he can no longer carry messages to Ted, she lashes him with her tongue. Leo, in tears, dashes off to the farmhouse with the message.

After the cricket match, Ted sings the Gilbert and Sullivan song "Take a pair of sparkling eyes", accompanied by Marian on the piano.

Ted, in an effort to calm the boy, tries to keep his promise to tell him about love. But he is clumsy, and ends up not really saying anything. Leo turns angrily on him, threatening once again not to carry his messages. Ted tells him curtly to get out. Leo, caught up in an intrigue of emotions he doesn't understand, resorts to the magic he renounced after the accident to his schoolchums. He waits up until midnight, then creeps out to the derelict summerhouse, uproots the belladonna and, once back in his room, begins to brew a potion from it to cast out "the evil".

Leo's 13th birthday begins badly with a rainstorm, and gets worse when Mrs Maudsley catches him

hiding a letter he has agreed to take to Ted,
provided Marian promises not to miss his birthday
party. Mrs Maudsley, furious, insists that Leo hand
her the letter. Leo manages to avoid doing so, but
Mrs Maudsley has already guessed its contents.
Marian, in her letter, has asked Ted to meet her just
before the party at which Leo's birthday cake is to
be cut. The afternoon is dark, with a thunderstorm
raging. When Marian fails to turn up, a carriage is
sent out to look for her. When it returns empty, Mrs
Maudsley seizes Leo angrily by the arm, saying: "You
know where she is."

Leo, not knowing what else to do, leads her to the
abandoned summerhouse. On their way they pass a
green bicycle, Marian's present to Leo – destined to
remain a present never given and a bicycle never
ridden. As Mrs Maudsley and the boy reach the
summerhouse, they see a shadow moving on the
wall ... inside they find Marian and Ted lying in each
other's arms ...

Some 60 years later, Leo Colston, who has never
married, calls on the widowed Marian, now Lady
Trimingham. She tells him that her grandson, who
looks very much like his grandfather (Ted), is in love

with a girl but won't marry her because he believes there is some sort of curse on his family. She begs the old man to tell the boy the whole story; to put his fears at rest. And once again, Leo finds himself acting as a "go-between".

Mrs Maudsley forces Leo to show her where the lovers are.

Reprinted from the 1971 publicity brochure of the film The Go-Between, *by permission of* Canal + Image UK Limited

The tragic outcome.

The Go-Between

Film Credits

Cast

Marian/Lady Trimingham	JULIE CHRISTIE
Ted Burgess	ALAN BATES
Leo Colston	DOMINIC GUARD
Mrs Maudsley	MARGARET LEIGHTON
Leo Colston as a man	MICHAEL REDGRAVE
Mr Maudsley	MICHAEL GOUGH
Viscount Trimingham	EDWARD FOX
Marcus	RICHARD GIBSON
Denys	SIMON HUME-KENDALL
Kate	AMARYLLIS GARNETT
Charles	ROGER LLOYD PACK
Ted Burgess's grandson	JOHN BATES
Butler	JOHN RICHIE
Under Butler	STEPHEN RANDALL
First Maid	JULIA HOWLETT
Second Maid	GERALDINE MOON
Between Maid	PAULINE WIFFEN
Housekeeper	MRS TATE
Cook	JOAN HARRISON
Second Cook	GERALDINE BIRD
Gardeners	GEORGE GRIEFF, CHARLES WINN
Coachman	NOBBY MITCHELL
Coachman	TREVOR BUXTON
House guests	KEITH BUCKLEY, JOHN REES, GORDON RICHARDSON
House guests (scenes 1–150)	VERONICA BEDFORD, LIZZIE HARVEY, PETER HOWARD, CLAIRE LASKO, ALEX NOVELL, MICHAEL ROBBINS
House guests (scenes 151–end)	SUSAN BRADLEY, JANE CLARKE, JAMES CRICK, MIRIAM RAWLINSON, WILLIAM STEBBINGS

Crew

Directed by	JOSEPH LOSEY
Produced by	JOHN HEYMAN, NORMAN PRIGGEN
Screenplay by	HAROLD PINTER
Based on the novel *The Go-Between* by	L.P. HARTLEY
Executive Producer	ROBERT VELAISE
Music composed and conducted by	MICHEL LEGRAND
Director of Photography	GERRY FISHER, B.S.C.
Art Director	CARMEN DILLON
Assistant Art Director	TESSA DAVIES
Assistant Art Director	MARTIN GASCOIGNE
Editor	REGINALD BECK
Production Supervisor	DENIS JOHNSON JNR.
Location Manager	JOHN SOUTHWOOD
Costume Designer	JOHN FURNISS
Costume Co-ordinator	CAMILLA FARMER

Titles by	RICHARD MacDONALD
Sound Recordists	PETER HANDFORD, HUGH STRAIN
Dubbing Editor	GARTH CRAVEN
1st Assistant Director	RICHARD DALTON
2nd Assistant Director	TERENCE HODGKINSON
3rd Assistant Director	GERRY GAVIGAN
Camera Operator	DUDLEY LOVELL
Focus Puller	MIKE RUTTER
Clapper Loader	STEPHEN SMITH
Camera Grip	PETER WOOD
Sound Camera Operator	G. (PAT) LEE
Boom Operator	DAVID STEPHENSON
Continuity	PAMELA DAVIES
Wardrobe Supervisor	EILEEN SULLIVAN
Wardrobe Master	KEN LAWTON
Chief Make-Up	BOB LAWRANCE
Make-Up Artiste	PHIL LEAKEY
Chief Hairdresser	STEPHANIE KAYE
Hairdresser	GLADYS LEAKEY
Production Accountant	BARRY DAVIS
Assistant Accountant	CHRIS CHRISAFIS
Construction Manager	TONY MORRIS
Production Buyer	DENNIS MADDISON
S/B Carpenter	J. HORNE
S/B Stage Hand	W. TESTER
C/H Prop	REX HOBBS
Prop	BRIAN LOFTHOUSE
Prop	BRIAN WHEELER
S/B Painter	H.D. WALTERS
S/B Rigger	A.T. LOWEN
Supervising Electrician	DAVID EADES
Projectionist	ROBERT LEE
Unit Publicist	HUGH SAMPSON
Publicity Secretary	APRIL BRANDON
Stills Photographer	NORMAN HARGOOD
Producer's Secretary	SALLY O'BRIEN
Costumes executed by	NATHANS
Cricket equipment by	SLAZENGER'S
Industry Observer	WARREN BEATTY

SOURCES

Manuscript sources
JWL
Joseph Losey Archive, British Film Institute

HPP
Harold Pinter Papers, British Library,
Add. 88880/2/42-44

PL
Patricia Losey, unpublished diary

RHP
Sir Roy Harrod Papers, British Library,
Add. 71184

Printed sources
Bailey
John Bailey: "How can I ever forget?"
Eastern Daily Press, July 11, 1995

Bednerik
Marya Bednerik: "The ecology of *The Go-Between*", in Steven H. Gale, ed., *The Films of Harold Pinter* (SUNY, New York, 2001)

Billington, *Go-Between*
Michael Billington: "Losey's Go-Between",
Illustrated London News, July, 1971

Billington, *Pinter*
Michael Billington: *The Life and Work of Harold Pinter* (Faber & Faber, London, 1996)

Boorman
John Boorman: *Money into Light: The Emerald Forest: A Diary* (Faber & Faber, London, 1985)

Caute
David Caute: *Joseph Losey: Revenge on Life* (Faber & Faber, London, 1994)

Ciment
Michel Ciment: *Conversations with Losey* (Methuen, London and New York, 1985)

Cocks
Jay Cocks: "Two by Losey", *Time*, August 9, 1971

Delfont
Bernard Delfont with Barry Turner: *East End, West End* (Macmillan, London, 1990)

De Rham
Edith de Rham: *Joseph Losey* (André Deutsch, London, 1991)

Ewbank and Hildred
Tim Ewbank and Stafford Hildred: *Julie Christie: The Biography* (André Deutsch, London, 2001)

Forbes
Bryan Forbes: *A Divided Life: Memoirs* (Heinemann, London, 1992)

Fox
Angela Fox: *Slightly Foxed by My Theatrical Family* (Isis, Oxford, 1987)

Fry
Stephen Fry: *Moab is My Washpot* (Hutchinson, London, 1997)

Gardner
Colin Gardner: *Joseph Losey* (Manchester University Press, 2004)

Gow
Gordon Gow: "Weapons: Joseph Losey in an interview with Gordon Gow", *Films and Filming*, October, 1971

Harrod
Wilhelmine, Lady Harrod: "Norfolk and the Go-Between", in the official programme to the royal screening, Norwich, October, 1971

Hayward
Anthony Hayward: *Julie Christie* (Robert Hale, London, 2000)

Hirsch
Foster Hirsch: *Joseph Losey* (Twayne Publishers, Boston, 1980)

Kulik
Karol Kulic: *Alexander Korda: The Man Who Could Work Miracles* (W.H. Allen, London, 1975)

Meredith
Anthony Meredith: *Richard Rodney Bennett: The Complete Musician* (Omnibus Press, London, 2010)

Minney
R.J. Minney: *'Puffin' Asquith: The Biography of the Honourable Anthony Asquith, Aesthete, Aristocrat, Prime Minister's Son and Film Maker* (Leslie Frewin, London, 1973)

Norfolk Fair
"Melton Constable Hall: A visit to the film set of the Go-Between and a history of the Hall", *Norfolk Fair*, December, 1970

Palmer and Riley
James Palmer and Michael Riley, *The Films of Joseph Losey* (Cambridge University Press, 1993)

Renton
Linda Renton, *Pinter and the Object of Desire, An Approach through the Screenplays* (Legenda, Oxford, 2002)

Spoto
Donald Spoto: *Otherwise Engaged: The Life of Alan Bates* (Arrow, London, 2008)

Taylor
John Russell Taylor: "The Go-Between", *Sight and Sound*, vol. 39, no. 4, Autumn, 1970, pp. 202–3

Tolhurst
Peter Tolhurst: *East Anglia, A Literary Pilgrimage*, foreword by Elspeth Barker (Black Dog Books, Norwich, 1998)

Usborne
Richard Usborne: "My Blandings Castle", *Blackwood's Magazine*, vol. 312, no. 1885, November, 1972

Wills, *Naked*
Anneke Wills, *Naked* (Hirst Books, Andover, 2009)

Wills, *Self Portrait*
Anneke Wills: *Self Portrait* (Hirst Books, Andover, 2007)

Wilson
Angus Wilson, ed., *Writers of East Anglia* (Secker & Warburg, London, 1977)

Wood
Trevor Wood: "A Noble House Reborn", *House and Garden*, December, 1970

Wright
Adrian Wright: *Foreign Country: The Life of L.P. Hartley* (André Deutsch, London, 1996)

INDEX

Endpapers:

*A letter written by the thirteen-year-old
Leslie Hartley to his mother in 1909,
describing his stay at Bradenham Hall,
Norfolk: "We always have late dinner
here. There is going to be a cricket
match today, the Hall against the
village". Years later, Hartley found the
letter among his mother's papers and
saw in it the germ of a story that was to
become The Go-Between, the novel he
published in 1953.*